A WORLD OF FLA

Thailand

A WORLD OF FLAVOURS

Thailand

Authentic regional recipes

Christine Watson

APPLE

A Quintet Book

First published in the UK in 2009 by
Apple Press
7 Greenland Street
London NW1 0ND
United Kingdom

www.apple-press.com

Cover photo © FoodPhotogr. Eising / Stockfood America

ISBN: 978 1 84543 320 8
QTT.WFTH

This book was conceived, designed and produced by
Quintet Publishing Limited
6 Blundell Street
London N7 9BH
United Kingdom

Project Editors: Joe Fullman, Martha Burley
Designer: Rod Teasdale
Art Director: Michael Charles
Managing Editor: Donna Gregory
Publisher: James Tavendale
Additional Text: Camilla Barton, Diana Craig

Printed and bound in Singapore

10 9 8 7 6 5 4 3 2 1

Contents

Introduction 6

Classic Dishes 26

Northern Thailand 84

Northeastern Thailand 104

Central Thailand 126

Southern Thailand 172

Index 222

Introduction

Thai cooking is all about harmony: achieving the perfect balance between the five flavours – sweet, sour, hot, salty and bitter. This book contains more than a hundred recipes from all over Thailand, from rich green and red curries to hot and sour soups and spicy seafood salads. What they all have in common is an emphasis on fresh ingredients, usually cooked quickly so as to retain their zest and bite. These recipes showcase both the Thais' own culinary inventiveness and the influence of foreign cuisines. Over the centuries the country's cooks have appropriated ingredients from across Asia – fiery spices from India, noodles from China and peanut sauces from Indonesia – which have been adapted to produce new and original recipes.

ABOVE: Flat cabbage, Indian lettuce, a-choy and bok choy for sale at a Thai market.

LEFT: A beach restaurant on the Thai island of Koh Chang.

The regions of Thailand

ABOVE: Thailand's floating markets are among the most photographed destinations in the country. Boats laden with a wide variety of tropical fruits, flowers and vegetables were once the mainstay of daily trading in the country.

Thailand is divided into four basic regions – north, northeast, centre and south. Though all have a shared culinary heritage, there are marked differences between the regions' cuisines. Some of these differences are purely practical. Ingredients necessarily vary from place to place according to climate and geography. In the tropical south, coconuts are a mainstay of many sauces, but they feature little in the cooler north where tomatoes are used instead. Seafood is popular in the centre and south, which both have extensive coastlines, but is largely absent from the landlocked north and northeast where meat, particularly pork, beef and chicken, is preferred.

Other differences are more subjective. Over time the peoples of the various region have developed clear preferences regarding the spice levels of their food. Northerners favour salty tastes above all others. In the northeast and south they tend to opt for hot and sour ones, while in the centre sweet flavours are popular.

Foreign influence has played an important role in establishing these trends. Thailand is bordered by Burma to the west and north, Laos to the east, Cambodia to the southeast and Malaysia to the south. All have had some degree of input into Thailand's culinary development, as have Vietnam, Indonesia and, particularly, China, which lies less than 100 kilometres (60 miles) from Thailand's northern border. It is from the Chinese that the Thais have inherited a love of noodles and the technique of cutting up their ingredients very small, so as to reduce the cooking time. As a result, few Thai dishes require the use of a knife. Instead, most meals are eaten using a fork and a spoon – with the fork used to push the food on to the spoon, the main eating implement.

One thing that does unite the country is rice, which is the basic staple of most meals, although, again, not all Thai people eat the same type of rice. In the centre and south, steamed, fragrant rice – also known as jasmine rice – is preferred, while in the north and northeast sticky rice is favoured, which is rolled into balls and dipped into sauces with the fingers.

There are no courses in a typical Thai meal. Rather, all the dishes – the soup, curry, salad, condiments, vegetables and rice – are served at the same time, the idea being to ensure harmony and balance, not just within each invidual dish, but throughout the entire meal.

BURMA

LAOS

Chiang Rai Province

Mae Hong Son Province

Phayao Province

Nan Province

Chiang Mai Province

Lampang Province

Lamphun Province

Phrae Province

Nong Khai Province

Nakhon Phanom Province

Uttaradit Province

Loei Province

Udon Thani Province

Sakon Nakhon Province

Nong Bua Lam Phu Province

Khon Kaen Province

Kalasin Province

Mukdahan Province

Sukhothai Province

Tak Province

Phitsanulok Province

Kamphaeng Phet Province

Phichit Province

Phetchabun Province

Chaiyaphum Province

Maha Sarakham Province

Roi Et Province

Yasothon Province

Amnat Charoen Province

Ubon Ratchathani Province

THAILAND

Nakhon Sawan Province

Uthai Thani Province

Chai Nat Province

Lop Buri Province

Nakhon Ratchasima Province

Buri Ram Province

Surin Province

Si Sa Ket Province

Sing Bori Province

Ang Thong Province

Kanchanaburi Province

Suphan Buri Province

Saraburi Province

Nakhon Pathom Province

Nontaburi Province

Prachin Buri Province

Sa Kaeo Province

Nakhon Nayok Province

Ratchaburi Province

Chachoengsao Province

CAMBODIA

Samut Songkhram Province

Phetchaburi Province

Chon Buri Province

Rayong Province

Chanthaburi Province

Prachuap Khiri Khan Province

Trat Province

Samut Prakan Province

Bangkok Metropolis Province

VIETNAM

Pathum Thani Province

Phra Nakhon Si Ayutthaya Province

Samut Sakhon Province

Chumpon Province

Ranong Province

Surat Thani Province

Phangnga Province

Krabi Province

Nakhon Si Thammarat Province

Phuket Province

Phatthalung Province

Trang Province

Pattani Province

Satun Province

Songkhla Province

Narathiwat Province

Yala Province

Northern Thailand

ABOVE: A rainbow in the mist-covered mountains of Pai, northern Thailand.

Thailand's northern region is high and mountainous with many forests. Its climate is a good deal cooler than the rest of the country, as are the tastes of its native inhabitants. Here, curries are generally mild with few spices. Salty tastes predominate, while sweet and sour ones are much less favoured.

Much of the region's land is given over to agriculture, particularly in the many river valleys where flooded fields produce the sticky rice that is the region's staple food, served as an accompaniment to almost all meals, including breakfast. Elsewhere, vegetables and fruit are grown in abundance, the region's cool climes allowing for the cultivation of certain crops, such as lychees and strawberries, which do not grow well in the rest of the country and form an important part of the local economy. Each year, the people of the north hold numerous festivals in honour of its many and various fruits. Pork dishes, such as nam prik ong (minced pork with chillies and tomatoes) are also very popular in the north – more so than those of any other meat – as are dishes featuring freshriver fish, but seafood, owing to the region's distance from the sea, is rarely consumed and usually only in dried form.

The region's largest city is Chiang Mai, which was once the capital of the ancient kingdom of Lanna. Located in the lush foothills of the Himalayas, the city remained largely isolated from the rest of the country until well into the twentieth century. As a result, its people maintain a proudly independent culture. At its numerous restaurants and street stalls – only Bangkok has more – visitors can sample many of the region's distinctive dishes, such as khao soi (curried noodles) and, a specialty of the city, sai ua, or Chiang Mai sausages, which are made from preserved pork and usually served with drinks accompanied by peanuts, ginger and chillies.

Family meals are traditionally eaten at a low table known as a kantoke, on to which are placed a succession of dishes, all eaten with sticky rice and an assortment of condiments. Today, elaborate kantoke dinners, often accompanied by traditional Lanna dancing, have become a popular tourist attraction.

RIGHT: Tea plantations in northern Thailand are popular tourist destinations.

Northeastern Thailand

ABOVE: Buddha statue in northeastern Thailand.

The I-san, as the northeast is known in Thailand, is the country's most populated region. Strangely, it's also the least fertile. The soils here are of a notoriously poor quality and much of the land is susceptible to flooding. As a result northeasterners have become masters at improvisation, making the most out of whatever they can find, and creating meals out of some rather unusual sources of protein, including geckos, grasshoppers and snails.

Of course, the people here do also eat more traditional choices, such as pork, chicken and beef, as well as fresh fish caught in the region's numerous rivers. These include the mighty Mekong, which marks the border between Thailand and neighbouring Laos, from where various dishes have found their way into the northeastern repertoire. One of the most popular is khanom bung, a spicy crêpe eaten on festive occasions.

Whatever the ingredients, northeasterners above all like their food strongly spiced and extremely hot. This is particularly evident in the region's most famous dish, larb, a potent blend of chopped raw meat – pork, beef, chicken or fish – and spices. Northeasterners also have a fondness for the sour taste of unripe green papaya, which features in one of the region's other well known recipes, som tam, where it is combined with chillies, fish sauce, garlic and peanuts to form a delightful mixture of fresh and hot flavours. The northeastern version of nam pla, the fish sauce that is a mainstay ingredient throughout the country, is renowned for its strength and pungency.

As with the north, evening meals are served on a large tray on to which are placed an array of dishes – soups, curries, salads – and a wicker basket of sticky rice. Almost all meals feature this rice, which is preferred to the steamed, fragrant varieties of the central and southern regions. But then, there is a plentiful supply, as it is one of the few crops suited to the northeast's flooded, poorly drained soils. In fact, the crop grows so well here that the region can sometimes support two rice harvests a year.

RIGHT: A fisherman casts his net in one of the region's numerous rivers.

Central Thailand

ABOVE: Dried spices and nuts are just a taster of what is on offer in the markets in Bangkok.

Home to both Bangkok, the modern Thai capital, and Ayutthaya, the former capital, central Thailand has perhaps the richest heritage of any of the country's regions. Sometimes known as the 'heart' of Thailand, it was the development of rice production in the region's vast central plain that powered the expansion of the Thai state from the thirteenth century onward. It is still the country's primary rice basket, although today its fertile soils also produce a wealth of fresh fruit and vegetables. Fish and seafood, caught by an army of fishing boats scouring the Gulf of Thailand, are also popular.

In central Thailand, high and low cuisine exist in perfect harmony. At one end of the scale are the elaborate fruit and vegetable carvings that adorn many tables, a continuation of a tradition first established by cooks preparing meals for the royal family at Bangkok's Grand Palace. At the other is an abundance of simple Thai street food with Bangkok, in particular, home to a plethora of stalls selling cheap bowls of noodles, Thai-style omelettes and sizzling seafood fritters.

Many of Thailand's best-known dishes, including green and red curries, and the hot and sour soups known as tom yum, originated in central Thailand, from where they have spread all over the globe. This is also where many of the signature Thai seasonings – garlic, ginger, black pepper and chilli – were first used. As influential as the region has been, however, it's never been averse to seeking inspiration from elsewhere. As the centre of the country's economy, it has long acted as a magnet for migrants from other regions (and beyond) who have brought with them their own culinary traditions to add to the general pot. Indeed, the tastes of the people of the central region, who prefer their food mildly spiced with a hint of sweetness, can – along with their fondness for noodles (eaten in greater volume here than anywhere else in the country) – probably be traced back to the influence of the Chinese who boast one of the region's largest immigrant populations.

RIGHT: Thai fruit carving demonstrates the artistry and elegance of the region's culinary tradition.

Southern Thailand

ABOVE: Fresh fish drying out in the sun is a common sight on the beautiful beaches of southern Thailand.

Thailand's southern region consists of a long, narrow peninsula of land and several islands, the largest and most famous of which is the popular holiday destination of Phuket – although, today, Phuket is actually linked to the mainland by a bridge. With so many of the region's settlements lying on or near the coast, the people have become experts in harvesting the bounty of the sea, with more fish and seafood eaten here than in any other region. This is prepared in a variety of ways. Grilling is perhaps the most popular option, but fish stir-fries and salads are also widely eaten, as is fish curry, the recipe for which has been derived from neighbouring Malaysia.

One of the region's other mainstays, satay with peanut sauce, is also of foreign origin, having travelled to Thailand, via Malaysia, from Indonesia. Meat is perhaps less popular than in other regions, partly as a result of the wealth of fish alternatives and partly because of the influence of the many Muslim communities living in the southern end of the region for whom the eating of pork is forbidden. However, massaman curry, a Muslim dish made of beef, peanuts, cardamom, tamarind juice and coconut milk, is another mainstay of southern Thai restaurant menus.

The south enjoys Thailand's warmest, lushest climate, providing the perfect growing conditions for coconuts, which crop up in all manner of local recipes. The fruit's milk and cream form the basis of many curries, its oil is used for frying, while the dried, grated flesh is employed as a sort of all-purpose condiment to enhance everything from salads and soups to desserts.

Despite their fondness for coconut and the many other tropical fruits that grow in such abundance here, southern Thais are by no means sweet-toothed. In fact they are renowned for producing the hottest curries in the whole country. Southern Thai cooks like to use a lot of spices and produce fiery recipes that will test the fortitude of even the most iron-tongued of travellers.

RIGHT ABOVE: The island of Kho Phi Phi at sunset.
RIGHT BELOW: The islands in the Andaman Sea, to the southeast of Thailand, have a lush and green terrain.

Techniques and equipment used in Thai cooking

ABOVE: Stir-frying is one of the most popular methods of cooking in Thailand.

The best Thai cooking does not depend on precise quantities or strictly adhered-to recipes but is traditionally a more inventive process, with cooks using the finest of whatever ingredients are in season or close to hand. The result is an imaginative, extremely varied cuisine, consisting of composite dishes made up of an assortment of many different ingredients.

In the Thai kitchen, much of the work goes into the initial preparation of the ingredients. Meat and vegetables are cut up into small pieces so that they will cook quickly and evenly when stir-fried – one of the most popular methods of cooking. Smaller pieces also mean more surface area to coat with spices and other flavourings, which makes for a tastier dish. Another reason why ingredients are cut into bite-sized pieces is that knives were not traditionally used at the table. Diners could thus not cut their food up and ate instead with their fingers – perhaps scooping handfuls from a banana-leaf 'bowl' – so the pieces had to be of manageable size.

For stir-frying, deep-frying and other methods of cooking, a wok is essential – no Thai kitchen would be without one. Both frying pan and saucepan rolled into one, this vital piece of equipment should ideally be made of stainless steel, as this heats quickly and evenly. A good spatula, either stainless steel or wood, is also necessary for stirring and turning the food as it cooks. Frying in a wok is best done over a gas flame as the heat is more instant and controllable than on an electric hob. As well as being stir-fried, strips or small pieces of meat may also be blanched or braised, for serving with noodles, or skewered and grilled, as in satay.

A traditional clay pot – available in Asian stores – is another useful piece of equipment in the Thai kitchen. Topped with a lid, this heats slowly and holds the heat well, and may be used for making soups and sauces.

As rice is such a staple in the Thai diet, great care is taken in cooking it. Depending on the variety, it will either be rinsed thoroughly or soaked for several hours to remove excess starch. The traditional method for cooking rice is to steam it, wrapped in muslin, in a bamboo or reed basket over a container of boiling water. Modern technology has

LEFT: A mortar and pestle is useful to make red chilli paste – a key ingredient in many Thai recipes.

come to the cook's aid, and there are now electric rice steamers that make the job foolproof. After steaming, the rice could be chilled overnight for additional frying the following day. Note that care must be taken to chill the rice quickly after first cooking, as *bacillus cereus,* a bacteria that can cause food poisoning, can withstand the boiling process and will start to germinate at room temperature. To be safe, always serve rice as soon as it has been cooked, or cool leftover rice as soon as possible and store in a fridge for no more than a day.

Although a food processor now tackles many of the jobs in the Thai kitchen, some dishes demand a mortar and pestle. A heavy stone one is a good all-round tool, used for anything from making curry paste to pounding garlic. Where a lighter touch is required – for example, for bruising papaya for green papaya salad – a traditional clay mortar and pestle is a better choice.

ABOVE: Kaffir lime leaves are widely used in Thai cooking for their unmistakably citrus scent and flavour.

Key ingredients of the Thai kitchen

Thai cooks have many ingredients at their disposal in their search for the right balance of the five flavours – salty, sweet, sour, bitter and hot. Perhaps the saltiest of all Thai ingredients is nam pla. Made by fermenting anchovies in brine, then drawing off the liquid, this thin, brown, fishy sauce is a culinary essential. Sweetness may come from the natural sugars in foods, but for extra sweetness – for example, in desserts – Thai cooks use coconut or palm sugar. Oils from the same palms are used for frying.

To add tartness to a dish, a cook might use the sour, fleshy seeds of the tamarind tree, which has become a staple of Thai cuisine since its introduction from India. Other souring agents include the leaves, peel and zest of the kaffir lime, a tropical citrus fruit, and the more delicately flavoured lemongrass, with its lemony fragrance. Herbs and green vegetables supply most of the bitter flavour in Thai food. One especially bitter food – loved by Thais but an acquired taste for Westerners – is the bitter melon.

Spices, such as chillies, supply Thai food with its hot, pungent flavours. The most commonly used chillies in Thai cuisine are from the *Capsicum annuum* species. Prik kee noo (also known as bird's eye or Thai chillies) point downwards from the plant and their colours change directly from green to red. Despite their size, these peppers are surprisingly hot. Prig lang chillies are a dried variety which are largely used for curry paste. If you find it hard to get hold of Thai ones, serrano chillies are a great alternative. Found fresh or toasted, they are often used in green sauces. Another choice for Thai cuisine could be jalapeños, as they are similarly hot. Pasilla chillies (also known as black chillies) are popular in Thai cooking, and are normally found dried or powdered. Their sweet, dark and smoky aroma lends a wonderfully rich flavour to sauces. Galangal (also known as khaa or lengkuas root) is a member of the ginger family, and imparts its fresh spiciness to seafood dishes, soups and salads when pounded to a paste; it is also indispensable in Thai curries. Another culinary essential, which again found its way into Thailand via Indian cooking, is turmeric. Mild in taste but strong in colour, it turns any food to which it is added a bright orangey-yellow.

Other popular flavouring ingredients include two herbs – the sweetly scented leaves of coriander, and Thai basil, which releases its full aniseed-like flavour only when cooked. Pandanus leaf, also known as bai toey, is used to flavour desserts, being second in popularity only to jasmine.

Thais eat plenty of meat, including pork, beef, chicken and duck. Fish and seafood are also popular, either served whole (typically grilled), as part of a curry or noodle dish, or used in such condiments as oyster sauce or shrimp paste.

As elsewhere in Asia, rice is a staple food in Thailand. Thai cooks can choose from white sticky rice, which is most common in northern and northeastern Thailand, where it replaces the plain steamed fragrant rice (also known as jasmine rice) of the central and southern regions. Rice is also used to make noodles and flour. Roti, a flat, pan-fried bread, is a Thai favourite too, especially in the Muslim south. It is usually served as a sweet snack, dripping with condensed milk or stuffed with banana, but it may be savoury too.

Coarsely ground peanuts are combined with other ingredients to make dipping sauces to accompany satay (meat skewers) and fried tofu cubes. A sprinkling of ground peanuts also accompanies that popular Thai dish, pad thai.

As Thailand is not a dairy-producing country, coconut milk and cream are used instead of cow's milk to add creaminess to sauces and desserts.

RIGHT: Dried prig lang chillies are commonly used in chilli paste.

ABOVE: Pad thai uses the contrasting textures of mushrooms, bean sprouts and coriander and marries them with sweet, sour and salty sauces. See page 64 for recipe.

Iconic Thai dishes

Pad thai

One of the country's most famous gastronomic exports, pad thai is a delicious and deceptively simple stir-fry of flat rice-stick noodles mixed with a sauce made of sugar (for sweetness), tamarind juice (for sourness), and fish sauce (for saltiness). This is then combined with a host of other ingredients, which may include eggs, chillies, bean sprouts, garlic, shallots, spring onions and ginger, plus an optional source of protein – chicken, pork, beef, shrimp, fish, tofu, etc. Ingredients and quantities change from region to region, and from kitchen to kitchen. It's up to the cook to choose which ingredients and flavours will work best together. Experience and improvisation based on what's available are the key to creating a good pad thai. It is an extremely versatile dish that works equally well as part of a main meal or as a quick snack. In Thailand it's a popular street food.

Though today synonymous with Thai cooking – the name means 'Thai-fried noodles' – the dish is actually believed to be of Vietnamese origin. It was popularized in Thailand via a propoganda campaign organized by Prime Minister Luang Pibulsongram during the Second World War. Concerned that the population's growing rice consumption might have an impact on rice exports – the country's principal source of revenue – he encouraged the Thai people to swap to eating noodles by portraying pad thai as a 'national' dish and the eating of it as a sign of patriotism. Pibulsongram was eventually ousted in a coup, but his culinary gift to the nation continues to thrive today.

Colour-coded curries

No Thai menu would be complete without a choice of green, red or yellow curries. Their respective colours are down to the curry paste that forms the basis of the recipe. Green curries use fresh green chillies, red curries use fresh (or more commonly dried) red chillies, while yellow curries use either red or yellow chillies mixed with turmeric. These are blended with lemongrass, galangal, garlic, shallots, kaffir lime, coriander and shrimp paste to form the paste. To make the curry, the paste is fried with aubergine, shallots, Thai basil leaves, kaffir lime and some sort of meat, fish or seafood, and then cooked in coconut milk. The heat level of the curry depends on the ratio of curry paste to coconut milk. Yellow curry, most often eaten in the southern part of the country, is richer and creamier than the others, as it uses coconut cream as well as coconut milk.

Salads

Thailand is particularly renowned for its fresh salads, several of which, including som tam and yum nua, originated in the northeast, where they like their food hot and sour. Som tam is a spicy salad made with unripe green papayas that has become a nationwide favourite, sold on street stalls all over the country. Its combination of garlic, chillies, green tomatoes, green beans, shredded raw papaya, fish sauce, lime juice and palm sugar should be hot, sour and a little salty. Simple recipes which combine mango, chicken, chilli and rice in a palette of colors are typical of the Thai cuisine. Yum nua is a spicy beef salad that uses lime juice, fish sauce and chillies to dress tender strips of beef on a bed of coriander, salad leaves, onion, cucumber and tomatoes. It has been voted one of the ten most popular dishes with visitors to the country.

ABOVE: Som tam salad, with papaya and chilli, is a Thai favourite. See page 109 for recipe.

ABOVE: Many areas of the country hold annual fruit festivals during May. The lychee fair in Chiang Rai includes cooking competitions, parades and beauty contests in celebration of the fruit.

Festival foods

Sweets

The typical Thai dessert course is made up of a simple selection of fruit. Although the country does have a rich tradition of crafting elaborate sweets, known as khanom, these tend to be reserved for special occassions, such as the festival of Wan Awk Pans. This comes at the end of Vassa, a three-month period in the rainy season when Buddhist monks, and some members of the public, retreat to meditate, giving up worldy pleasures such as meat, alcohol and sweet foods. When the three months are up, illuminated boats carry offerings of kao tum mut – sticky rice sweets wrapped in banana leaves – to the monks to celebrate (and reward) the end of their period of self-denial.

Thai sweets are not just about indulgence. Many have symbolic significance and are used in ceremonies, such as weddings, or the commemoration of a new house, to bring luck. Some of these ritual sweets are golden-coloured (the colour is derived from egg yolk) which represents prosperity and wealth. Others have numerical significance, such as khanom chun (layered dessert), an elaborate confection made up of nine separate layers, nine being a lucky number in Thailand representing advancement and progress.

Fruit

Each year Thailand's northern district holds numerous festivals in honour of its many and various fruits, which make up one of the region's most important exports. May is the peak festival season, when the town of Fang marks the lychee harvest with parades and street fairs, while nearby San Sai holds beauty pageants and cooking competitions in honour of the mango. February sees the strawberry festival in Samoeng where a variety of strawberry-based treats – including even strawberry wine – can be bought, attracting visitors from all over Thailand and beyond.

Vegetarian festival

Perhaps the best-known Thai food festival is the annual celebration of vegetarian food, or kin jay, held in early October throughout the country and across Asia. The festival originated in China and is largely observed by Thai people of Chinese descent. It supposedly commemorates the period each year, during the ninth lunar month, when people's ancestors return briefly to earth to observe the behaviour of their descendents, in order to make sure they are living good lives in accordance with Buddhist teaching – which of course means refraining from eating meat. The whole thing could be seen as an exercise in 'putting on a front', so as not to disappoint the visiting ancestors, but it is nonetheless taken very seriously by many people. During the ten-day festival observers refrain from eating not just meat and fish, but any animal-derived product, including milk and eggs. Strong-smelling foods, such as garlic and onions, are also off-limits.

At this time street stalls with bright red and yellow signs announcing 'jay' (vegetarian food) for sale appear throughout the country. At home and at schools, soybean milk, noodles with mushrooms and tofu, plus lots of vegtables are consumed as meat and dairy subsitutes. Soy sauce is also used instead of fish sauce to create special versions of pad thai and red curry. Some households even use special kitchen utensils that have never been used to cook meat, so as to avoid the possibility of 'contamination'.

ABOVE: These bright Thai coconut sweets are special treats for the festive period.

CHAPTER ONE

Classic dishes

While each region of Thailand has its own distinctive cuisine, often influenced by the culinary history of its neighbouring countries, there are many recipes that enjoy nationwide appeal. Regional variations do still occur, of course. The emphasis on fresh ingredients that lies at the heart of all Thai cooking means that the recipe for something as widely eaten as pad thai will change from area to area according to the availability of local produce. It is this versatility that is perhaps the greatest triumph of Thai cooking. With most meals consisting of rice or noodles, accompanied by an assortment of other dishes, it is the perfect cuisine for laying on an elaborate, multi-course banquet, or for just rustling up something quick, easy and fresh-tasting after work.

LEFT: A floating market in Damnoen Saduak near Bangkok, Thailand. The abundance of fresh, local produce in Thailand contributes to the wonderful flavours and aromas in the cuisine.

Fish sauce with chillies

Ingredients
100 ml (4 fl. oz) fish sauce
10 fresh small green and red chillies, sliced
  into small circles
1 tsp sliced shallot
¼ tsp palm sugar (or dark muscovado sugar)
1 tbsp lime or lemon juice

Makes about 150 ml (6 fl. oz)

*K*nown as nam pla prik, this simple spicy sauce is found on tables throughout Thailand and is used to add both spiciness and saltiness to dishes. The fish sauce on which it is based is usually made from small fish, such as anchovies, which are then fermented using salt over many months to produce a rich, fragrant brew.

Mix all the ingredients together well. This is good for accompanying almost all Thai food, especially rice. Just sprinkle a little on your food to liven it up.

RIGHT: Nam pla prik is a quick and simple recipe which adds an authentic Thai feel to any noodle or rice dish.

Mango salsa

Ingredients
1 large ripe mango
1 small ripe pineapple
1 small red bell pepper, seeded and diced
4 spring onions, chopped

Makes 90 ml (3½ fl. oz)

*S*weet, tangy mango salsa makes a great accompaniment to fish or chicken dishes, providing a nice contrast to the hot and sour flavours of much Thai cooking.

Peel the mango, remove the stone and finely dice the flesh. Cut away the skin of the pineapple, remove the central core and dice the flesh.

Place all the ingredients in a serving dish and stir gently to combine. Cover and refrigerate for 1 hour before serving.

Chicken, aubergine and noodle broth

Ingredients

2 tbsp peanut oil

1 red pepper, seeded and finely chopped

2 garlic cloves, peeled and crushed

2 small white aubergines, cut into wedges

50 g (2 oz) pea aubergine, removed from their stalk

2 shiitake mushrooms, quartered

1 tbsp Thai red curry paste (see page 156)

2 tbsp tomato ketchup

50 ml (2 fl. oz) coconut cream

3 boneless chicken breasts, cut into bite-sized pieces

350 ml (12 fl. oz) chicken stock

2 tbsp light soy sauce

Juice of 1 lime

1 tsp raw sugar

175 g (6 oz) dried medium egg noodles, broken into short lengths

1 red chilli, finely shredded

Serves 4

FAR RIGHT: This small round variety of aubergine is also known as kermit aubergine. RIGHT: Pea aubergines are also known as devil's fig, or turkey berry.

*T*hai aubergines are very different from the large purple and black-skinned varieties common in the West. This recipe uses two different types of Thai aubergine – the small round variety, which has a pale green, almost white skin, and pea aubergines, which grow in small clusters and have a sharp, slightly bitter flavour.

In a wok, heat the peanut oil and stir-fry the red pepper and garlic for 3–4 minutes over a medium heat until the pepper is almost tender. Add the aubergine and shiitake mushrooms and cook for a further 2 minutes.

Add the Thai red curry paste and cook for 30 seconds. Stir in the tomato ketchup and coconut cream, cook for 1 minute, and then add the chicken, stock, light soy sauce, lime juice and sugar.

Simmer for 10 minutes. Meanwhile, cook the egg noodles in a saucepan of boiling water for 4 minutes. Drain and divide between four serving bowls. Spoon over the chicken stock and serve sprinkled with the shredded red chilli.

Spiced chicken soup

To save time, this recipe uses prepared satay sauce (or peanut butter) and pre-mixed Thai 7-spice seasoning, a blend of salt, chilli powder, garlic, ginger, coriander, lemon peel and black pepper, which can be found in most supermarkets.

Heat the oil in a large pan. Add the chicken and 7-spice seasoning and cook quickly until the chicken begins to brown. Stir in the lemongrass and potato, then add the stock and milk. Bring slowly to a boil, then cover and simmer for 20 minutes.

Stir in the spring onions and peas. Bring the soup to a boil and continue cooking for a further 5 minutes.

Add the satay sauce or peanut butter to the soup just before serving. Remove from the heat and stir until melted. Season to taste, and then serve garnished with a spoonful of double cream.

Ingredients

1–2 tbsp peanut or sunflower oil

2 small, skinless, boneless chicken breasts, shredded

2 tbsp Thai 7-spice seasoning

1 stick lemongrass, finely chopped

2 medium potatoes, diced

900 ml (1½ pints) chicken or vegetable stock

600 ml (1 pint) milk

3–4 spring onions, trimmed and finely sliced

75 g (3 oz) frozen peas

1–2 tbsp satay sauce or peanut butter

Salt and freshly ground black pepper

1–2 tbsp double cream, to garnish

Serves 4

RIGHT: The multi-coloured display of spices which make up the 7-spice seasoning. Each spice is readily available on the Damnoen Saduak floating markets in Thailand.

Clear soup with stuffed mushrooms

Ingredients

1.8 litres (3 pints) homemade clear stock, beef or chicken

18 small, dried shiitake mushrooms

1 small piece of winter melon

Stuffing for mushrooms:

225 g (8 oz) finely minced pork with a little pork fat

2 cloves garlic, crushed

4 stems of coriander, finely chopped with leaves chopped separately, plus extra leaves to garnish

Salt and freshly ground black pepper

2 tsp soy sauce

1 spring onion, trimmed and chopped

6 water chestnuts, peeled and chopped

Serves 8

The Asian mushrooms used in this recipe are most commonly known by their Japanese name, shiitake. In Thailand they are known as hed hom or fragrant mushrooms.

Prepare the stock or use a stock cube with a little soy sauce for colour. Soak the mushrooms for 30 minutes until soft. Remove the stalks and set aside.

Meanwhile prepare the stuffing for the mushrooms. Mix together the pork, garlic, coriander stems and leaves, seasoning, soy sauce, spring onion and water chestnuts. Divide the mixture between the soaked mushrooms. Place the stuffed mushrooms in a bamboo steamer over a wok with a sheet of greaseproof paper as a lid. Cook for 20 minutes.

While the mushrooms are cooking bring the stock to the boil. Add the cubes of melon and cook until just tender.

Place the stuffed mushrooms and a few cubes of melon in each serving bowl. Pour over the soup and scatter with a few coriander leaves.

Mini vegetable and herb rolls

*P*ad khad kow, also known as Chinese cabbage, features in many Thai recipes. When filling the rolls, it is important to remember not to pack them too tightly or they may burst open when plunged into the hot oil.

Heat 2 tablespoons of peanut oil in a wok and stir-fry the carrot, Chinese cabbage, celery, mushrooms and garlic for 2–3 minutes over a medium heat until just softened.

Stir in the celery leaves, chives and parsley and set aside to cool.

Lay the spring roll wrappers on a board and spoon a little of the filling onto each. Brush the edges of the wrappers with egg white and roll up from one corner to the opposite one, tucking in the sides and pressing the edges together to seal.

Heat the peanut oil to 180°C (350°F), or until a cube of bread dropped into it turns golden in 60 seconds. Fry the rolls in batches for about 3 minutes until golden brown. Drain on paper towel and serve hot with a dipping sauce.

Ingredients

2 tbsp peanut oil, plus extra for deep-frying
75 g (3 oz) grated carrot
75 g (3 oz) Chinese cabbage, finely shredded
2 sticks of celery, finely diced
50 g (2 oz) shiitake mushrooms, finely chopped
1 garlic clove, peeled and crushed
1 tbsp finely chopped celery leaves
1 tbsp snipped chives
1 tbsp chopped fresh parsley
13-cm (5-in) spring roll wrappers (squares of filo pastry)
1 egg white, lightly beaten

Serves 4

Spiced onions

These onions are only lightly cooked, to retain flavour and colour. This makes an excellent side dish with grilled fish. Total preparation and cooking time is just 15 minutes.

Heat the oil in a large frying pan or wok, then add the coriander seeds, lemongrass and chillies. Fry quickly for 1–2 minutes.

Add the sliced onions and the red onion to the pan and stir-fry quickly for approximately 2–3 minutes.

Add the spring onions and toss them in the juices. Heat for just a few seconds, then stir in the fish sauce. Add lime juice and salt to taste.

Serve the onions garnished with the shredded coconut and coriander.

Ingredients

2 tbsp peanut oil

1 tbsp coriander seeds

1 stalk lemongrass

1 green and 1 red chilli, seeded and finely chopped

2 large onions, thickly sliced

1 red onion, cut into 8 segments

10–12 spring onions, cut into 5-cm (2-in) pieces, finely sliced lengthways

2 tbsp fish sauce

Lime juice and salt to taste

Shredded coconut and coriander, to garnish

Serves 4

Lime-marinated pork skewers

*C*hicken could be substituted for the pork if you prefer. When slicing the lime leaf to make the dipping sauce, use small sharp scissors or a knife – if the slices are not wafer thin they will be unpleasant to eat.

To make the dipping sauce, stir the ingredients together until the sugar dissolves. Set aside for at least 1 hour to allow the flavours to develop.

Meanwhile, prepare the skewers. Mix the garlic, lime juice, sugar, fish sauce, soy sauce, and lemongrass and ginger purées together in a bowl, stirring until the sugar dissolves.

Add the pork and stir so the cubes are well coated. Cover and leave in a cool place to marinate for 1–2 hours.

Drain the pork and carefully thread the cubes onto the skewers. Grill or barbecue the skewers for 5 minutes, turning them over once or twice and brushing with any marinade left in the bowl.

Serve the skewers hot with the dipping sauce.

Ingredients

Dipping sauce:
3 tbsp light soy sauce
1 kaffir lime leaf, very finely sliced
1 tbsp fish sauce
Juice of 1 lime
1 tsp raw sugar
1 green chilli, seeded and finely sliced

Skewers:
3 large garlic cloves, peeled and crushed
Juice of 3 limes
1 tbsp granulated brown sugar
1 tbsp fish sauce
1 tbsp light soy sauce
1 tsp fresh lemongrass purée
½ tsp fresh ginger purée
450 g (1 lb) lean pork steaks, cut into 2.5-cm (1-in) cubes

Serves 4

Vegetable fritters with chilli relish

The quantities given for the relish will make more than is needed for the recipe, but any leftovers can be stored in a screw top jar in the refrigerator for up to two weeks.

To make the chilli relish, soak the red chillies in hot water for 30 minutes. Drain, cut open and remove the seeds. Pat dry on paper towels. Heat the peanut oil to 180°C (350°F), or until a cube of bread dropped into it turns golden in 60 seconds. Deep-fry the chillies for 2–3 minutes. Drain on paper towels. Transfer 2 tablespoons of the peanut oil to a wok and fry the green pepper and shallots for 5 minutes over a medium heat. Add the garlic, fry for 2 minutes and then stir in the tomatoes, green chillies and shrimp paste.

Lower the heat and simmer gently for 30 minutes. Cool a little and then purée in a food processor with the sugar and fish sauce. Return the purée to the wok and cook very gently for about 40 minutes until dark, caramelized and thick, stirring frequently so it does not stick to the wok and burn.

To make the fritters, mix together the mangetout peas, spring onions, sweetcorn, green pepper, crunchy peanut butter, fish sauce, sugar and mint. Stir in the flour, then the beaten egg to bind the mixture together.

Reheat the peanut oil to 180°C (350°F) for deep-frying. Drop tablespoons of the mixture into the hot oil and fry for 3–4 minutes until golden brown. Drain and serve hot, garnished with the lemon wedges and mint leaves and accompanied by the chilli relish.

Ingredients

For the chilli relish:
15 g (½ oz) large dried red chillies
Peanut oil for deep-frying
1 green pepper, seeded and chopped
4 shallots, peeled and chopped
2 garlic cloves, peeled and finely chopped
100 g (8 oz) chopped tomatoes
1 tsp shrimp paste
2 tbsp raw sugar
100 ml (4 fl. oz) fish sauce

For the fritters:
8 mangetout peas, finely chopped
2 spring onions, finely chopped
100 g (4 oz) sweetcorn kernels
½ green pepper, finely chopped
1 tbsp crunchy peanut butter
1 tbsp fish sauce
1 tsp white sugar
1 tbsp chopped fresh mint
75 g (3 oz) plain flour
1 egg, beaten

To garnish:
Lemon wedges
Mint leaves

Serves 4–6

Stir-fried greens

*P*ossibly the fastest dish to cook in Thailand, this is properly made with the water plant variously known as swamp cabbage, water cabbage, morning glory, ung choy or water convolvulus.

Heat the oil in a wok or frying pan until it is very hot.

Carefully add all the ingredients at once (watch for splattering), and quickly stir-fry for about 2 minutes.

Serve accompanied by steamed rice, or chicken, aubergine and noodle broth (page 31).

Ingredients
3 tbsp peanut or corn oil
300 g (11 oz) swamp cabbage leaves and
   stems, cut into 10-cm (4-in) lengths
100 ml (4 fl. oz) chicken stock
2 tbsp marinated soybeans
1 tbsp garlic, chopped

Serves 4–6

Thai hors d'oeuvre

A hard-to-find treat in Thailand, but always enjoyed. The Thais use fresh tree and vine leaves, but lettuce does just as well. You may need to soak the leaves in hot water for 2–3 minutes to aid their flexibility.

For the sauce, preheat the oven to 180°C (350°F). Roast the coconut, shrimp paste, galangal and shallots for 5 minutes until fragrant. Leave to cool. Place with the peanuts, shrimp and root ginger in a blender or food processor and blend together into a fine mixture.

Transfer the mixture to a heavy-bottomed pan with the sugar and water, mix well and bring to a boil. Simmer until it is reduced to about 150 ml (5 fl. oz). Remove from the heat and leave to cool.

To serve, first pour the sauce into a serving bowl and arrange all the ingredients in separate piles on a platter or in small bowls.

When everything is prepared, take a vine or lettuce leaf and place a small amount of each of the garnishes in the middle. Top with a spoonful of sauce and fold up into a little package. Repeat until you have the desired number of packages.

Ingredients

5 tbsp unsweetened grated coconut
3 tbsp shallots, finely diced
3 tbsp lime juice
3 tbsp fresh root ginger, diced
3 tbsp dried shrimp, chopped
3 tbsp unsalted roasted peanuts
2 tsp fresh small green chillies, chopped
1 bunch of edible vine leaves or lettuce

For the sauce:
2 tbsp unsweetened grated coconut
½ tbsp shrimp paste
½ tsp galangal, sliced
½ tsp sliced shallot
3 tbsp unsalted peanuts, chopped
2 tbsp dried shrimp, chopped
1 tsp fresh root ginger, sliced
225 g (8 oz) palm sugar (or dark muscovado sugar)
175 ml (6 fl. oz) water

Serves 6–8

Thai vegetables

For this recipe you'll require a pressure cooker and a lot of care. Thai chillies (also known as bird's eye or prik kee noo chillies) are very hot indeed. Use sparingly unless you know that you can take the heat. Wear rubber gloves when handling.

Heat the oil in the open cooker and sauté the garlic, lemongrass, root ginger, chillies and cinnamon stick for 2 minutes. Add the vegetables and sauté for 1 minute.

Pour in the coconut milk with 75 ml (3 fl. oz) of boiling water, then close the lid and bring to 7 kg (15 lb) pressure. Cook for 1 minute, then depressurize quickly and discard the lemongrass and cinnamon. Season and serve sprinkled with the chopped coriander.

For really crisp vegetables, bring to pressure then remove from the heat and depressurize quickly. For soft vegetables, pressure cook for 2 minutes.

Ingredients

1 tbsp sunflower oil

2–3 garlic cloves, peeled and crushed

2 lemongrass stalks (outer leaves discarded), bruised

1 small piece fresh root ginger, peeled and finely grated

1–2 Thai chillies (see page 20) or green jalapeño chillies, seeded and chopped

1 cinnamon stick, bruised

175 g (6 oz) broccoli florets

175 g (6 oz) cauliflower florets

2 carrots, peeled and chopped

1 large courgette, trimmed and cut into thick slices

100 g (4 oz) green beans, trimmed and halved

175 ml (6 fl. oz) coconut milk

Salt and freshly ground black pepper

1 tbsp chopped fresh coriander

Serves 4

Chicken, mango and rice salad

Ingredients

175 ml (6 fl. oz) water
1 tbsp fish sauce
½ tsp shrimp paste
1 tbsp raw sugar
1 tsp fresh lemongrass purée
Finely grated zest and juice of 1 lime
1 tbsp Thai basil, finely torn
450 g (1 lb) cooked rice, cooled
1 green mango, peeled, flesh cut away from
   the stone and thinly sliced
450 g (1 lb) cooked chicken meat, sliced
100 g (4 oz) beansprouts
100 g (4 oz) green beans, cooked
1 slice of pineapple, cut into small pieces
1 green chilli, finely sliced

Serves 4

Thai salads are hot and sour and use lots of fresh vegetables and herbs such as basil, chives and mint. Instead of chicken, this recipe can also be made with mixed seafood such as scallops, squid and shrimp.

Place the water in a saucepan with the fish sauce, shrimp paste, sugar, lemongrass purée, lime zest and juice and bring to a boil. Simmer for 2 minutes, then remove from the heat and stir in the basil. Set aside to cool.

Divide the rice between four cups or small bowls, pressing down so the rice is quite tightly packed, then turn out onto four serving plates.

Arrange the mango, chicken, beansprouts, green beans and pineapple around the rice and scatter over the green chilli. Spoon over a little of the dressing and serve the remainder separately.

Beef and rocket salad

*A*dd extra chilli powder if you like your dishes spicy, but only add half if you prefer your salads to be cool.

Mix together the chilli powder, ground coriander, black pepper and ginger. Roll the fillet in the spice mix until coated.

Heat the peanut oil in a heavy frying pan and seal the fillet on all sides until well browned. Allow to cool, then wrap tightly in cling film and place in the freezer for 30 minutes, to make it easier to slice later.

Remove the fillet from the freezer, unwrap and slice as thinly as possible.

Mix together the lemongrass, coriander, mint, fish sauce, rice vinegar, caster sugar and red chilli.

Once defrosted, arrange the fillet slices on a serving dish so that they overlap. Pile the rocket and chard leaves in the centre and spoon over the dressing. Scatter over the cashews, and serve garnished with the spring onions.

Ingredients

½ tsp chilli powder
1 tsp ground coriander
½ tsp ground black pepper
Pinch of ground ginger
450 g (1 lb) fillet of beef in
   one piece
1 tbsp peanut oil
½ tsp lemongrass purée
1 tbsp roughly chopped coriander
1 tbsp chopped mint leaves
1 tbsp fish sauce
2 tbsp rice vinegar
1 tsp caster sugar
1 red chilli, seeded and finely chopped
100 g (4 oz) rocket leaves
25 g (1 oz) red chard leaves
2 tbsp chopped cashews, lightly toasted
2 spring onions, shredded, to garnish

Serves 4

Green bean salad with shallot croûtons

Ingredients

For the chilli paste:

100 g (4 oz) shallots, finely chopped
1 tbsp chopped garlic
4 anchovy fillets
200 ml (8 fl. oz) water
2 tbsp sliced fresh ginger
2 tbsp sliced lemongrass
1 dried red chilli, seeded
1 tsp dried shrimp paste (optional)
Pinch of salt

For the salad:

220 g (8 oz) green beans
3 tbsp grated unsweetened coconut, fresh or
   desiccated
100 ml (4 fl. oz) peanut oil
6 garlic cloves, sliced 2-cm (⅛-in) thick
   lengthways
50 ml (2 fl. oz) fresh lime juice
50 ml (2 fl. oz) unsweetened coconut milk
1 tbsp red chilli paste (see above)
1 tbsp Thai fish sauce
1 tbsp sugar
12 whole radicchio leaves
2 serrano chillies (see page 20), preferably
   1 red and 1 green, seeded and chopped
Coriander sprigs, to garnish

For the shallot croûtons:

Peanut oil
4 medium shallots, sliced 2-cm (⅛-in) thick

Serves 4–6

*F*inely diced chicken breast or prawns, or a combination, can be added to this salad to make a hearty lunchtime or supper meal.

Mix the chilli paste ingredients together in a wok or pan, then cook over a medium heat for 1 minute. Allow to cool, before processing to a paste in a food processor.

Blanch the beans in a saucepan of boiling, salted water for about 3 minutes, until tender but still crisp. Drain and rinse under cold running water. Cut the beans into bite-sized pieces and set aside.

Heat a dry wok or small frying pan, add the grated coconut and toss gently for about 1 minute, until golden. Transfer the coconut to a plate.

Pour the peanut oil into the wok and heat to 180°C (375°F) using a deep-fat thermometer, or until a cube of bread dropped into the oil turns golden in 60 seconds. Remove the wok from the heat, add the garlic slices and stir until golden and crisp. Transfer the garlic to paper towel to drain.

In a bowl, whisk together the lime juice and coconut milk, then whisk in, one ingredient at a time, the chilli paste, fish sauce and sugar. Set aside. Make the shallot croûtons by heating the oil in a wok to 180°C (375°F). Remove the pan from the heat, add the shallots and stir for about 3 minutes, until the shallots are crisp and golden. Transfer to paper towel to drain. The shallots can be refrigerated, covered, for up to a week, but should then be lightly toasted on a baking sheet in the oven before using.

Arrange the radicchio leaves on a platter or individual plates. In a large bowl, combine the beans, the toasted coconut and the garlic slices. Pour the mixture of lime juice, coconut milk, chilli paste, fish sauce and sugar over the beans, coconut and garlic. Gently fold in the serrano chillies and serve garnished with coriander sprigs.

Rice salad with roasted coconut

*T*his is a classic leftover dish which can be made with rice from the night before. For health and safety reasons, do not use rice that has been chilled for more than 24 hours.

Preheat the oven to 180°C (350°F). Sprinkle the grated coconut on a baking sheet and roast the coconut for 5–8 minutes until brown and crisp.

Put the sauce ingredients in a pan, boil for 5 minutes, remove from the heat and strain.

Place the rice in half-cup moulds or large ramekins, press down, then invert onto a large serving platter. Arrange the remaining raw ingredients around the edge of the rice in separate groups. To eat, spoon some rice onto individual plates and take a little of each ingredient to mix with the rice according to taste. Spoon the sauce over the top.

Ingredients

For the salad:
100 g (4 oz) unsweetened grated coconut
225 g (8 oz) cooked rice, cooled
1 small pomelo or grapefruit, shredded
50 g (2 oz) dried shrimp, chopped
50 g (2 oz) bean sprouts
50 g (2 oz) lemongrass, finely sliced
25 g (1 oz) string beans, sliced
2 dried red chillies, pounded
1 tbsp kaffir lime leaf, finely shredded

For the sauce:
225 ml (8 fl. oz) water
2 tbsp anchovies, chopped
1 tbsp palm sugar (or dark muscovado sugar)
2 kaffir lime leaves, torn into small pieces
¼ tsp lemongrass, sliced

Serves 4

Noodles and Chinese leaves in a peanut dressing

Ingredients

For the salad:

450 g (1 lb) thin noodles

225 g (8 oz) mangetout peas

1 red pepper, cut into strips

1 medium cucumber, thinly sliced

4 spring onions, cut diagonally into thin slices

100 g (4 oz) Chinese leaves, shredded

For the peanut dressing:

100 g (4 oz) creamy peanut butter

100 ml (4 fl. oz) plain non-fat yogurt

1 tbsp soy sauce

1 garlic clove

2 tbsp dark sesame oil

3 tbsp chopped fresh coriander

2 tbsp rice wine vinegar

Serves 4

*T*he variety of textures in this dish is typical of Thai cuisine. The combination of soft noodles and crunchy vegetables in a nutty dressing ensures an exciting eating experience.

Cook the noodles in a large pan of boiling water according to the packet directions, until they are tender. Drain well, transfer to a large serving bowl and set aside. (If you are working ahead of time, toss with 1 tablespoon vegetable oil.)

Trim the stalk ends from the mangetout peas and blanch in boiling water for about 1 minute. Drain well and rinse in cold water – they should be bright green in colour. Add the mangetout peas, red pepper, cucumber and spring onions to the noodles. Add the Chinese leaves and toss again and serve.

To make the dressing, simply work the yoghurt into the peanut butter, then add all the other ingredients and mix well.

Chicken fried rice with onion and garlic

*O*ne of the basic standard Thai dishes, this always tastes best with rice from the day before – and is also much easier to cook if the rice has been chilled in the fridge overnight. For health and safety reasons, be careful and do not use rice which has been chilled for over 24 hours. In place of chicken, pork or shrimp are also commonly used.

Heat the oil in a wok or pan, add the chicken and garlic and mix well over the heat for 1 minute.

Add the onion and cook for another minute.

Break in the eggs, mix very well and then stir in the rice until it is piping hot.

Serve immediately accompanied by cucumber slices, tomato wedges, chopped spring onion and nam pla prik.

Ingredients

3 tbsp peanut or corn oil

200 g (7 oz) skinless, boneless chicken breasts, cut lengthwise into 1-cm (½-in) thick slices

1 tbsp chopped garlic

1 medium-sized onion, sliced

2 eggs

450 g (1 lb) cooked rice, chilled

½ cucumber, sliced

1 tomato, cut into 8 wedges

1 spring onion, chopped

5 tsp nam pla prik (fish sauce with chillies, see page 28)

Serves 4

Curried fried rice with green haricot beans

This recipe is all about balance – finding the perfect ratio of salty and sweet flavours to compliment the tender meats and crunchy vegetables. It's also a great way of using up any leftover rice and cooked meats. Galangal (Thai ginger or khaa root) adds a stronger flavour to the curry paste.

Cut the meats into fine slices, but leave the shrimp whole. Set the rice to one side. Wash, prepare and blanch the beans.

Using a mortar and pestle or food processor, grind together the chillies, shallots, garlic, lemongrass, galangal and coriander stems and peel. If using the chilli powder add it to these pounded ingredients. Heat the oil and fry this paste until it gives off a fragrant aroma.

Add the cooked meats and fry for around 1 minute. Add the rice, stirring all the time until the rice and the other ingredients are well mixed together. Add more oil if necessary to prevent the rice from sticking.

Season with salt, fish sauce and sugar to taste. Finally add the green beans. Serve garnished with coriander leaves.

Ingredients

225 g (8 oz) cooked meats, chicken, pork and
    shrimp
450 g (1 lb) cold, cooked long-grain rice
100 g (4 oz) green haricot beans, or long
    beans, cut into 5-cm (2-in) lengths and
    blanched
Fish sauce and sugar, to taste

For the curry paste:
3–5 dried red chillies, seeded, or 1–2 tsp chilli
    powder
6 shallots, finely chopped
2 cloves garlic, chopped
2 stems of lemongrass, from the bottom part
    of bulb, sliced
1 cm (½ in) galangal, finely sliced
4 stems of coriander, chopped, with the leaves
    reserved for garnish
2 tsp grated lime peel
6–8 tbsp vegetable oil

Serves 4–6

Chicken with Thai basil

Ingredients

450 g (1 lb) boneless, skinless chicken breasts,
  cubed
4 tbsp fish sauce
3 tbsp vegetable or sunflower oil
4 garlic cloves, peeled and sliced
2–4 red chillies, seeded and chopped
2 tsp dark soy sauce
½ tsp sugar
15 Thai basil leaves

Serves 4

*T*hai basil, known as bai jorapa or holy basil, has an aniseed flavour quite different from the sweet basil used in much Mediterranean cookery. Bunches of it can be found in many Asian food stores. Best served with steaming hot jasmine rice, this dish is popular throughout Southeast Asia.

Marinate the chicken in three tablespoons of the fish sauce and set aside for at least 30 minutes.

Heat the oil in a frying pan and fry the garlic and chillies until golden, which should take about about 2–3 minutes.

Add the chicken and fry until it starts to turn brown, which again should take around 2–3 minutes.

Add the remaining fish sauce, soy sauce and sugar. Stir for about 3–4 minutes or until well cooked.

Finally stir in the basil leaves, cook for a further 1 minute and serve immediately.

LEFT: Soy sauce is popular throughout Asia, and styles vary from country to country. Apart from the ubiquitous soy sauce, soy beans are made into a variety of stir-fry and cooking sauces. In Thai cuisine, a thin soy sauce works best, or black bean and yellow bean varieties.

Barbecue chicken with chilli vinegar sauce

If it is not the right time of year for a barbecue, the chicken can be cooked under a conventional grill or in a ridged pan. Serve with sticky rice (page 86) or fragrant rice (page 128).

Place the chicken breasts side by side in a shallow dish. Mix together the light soy sauce, fish sauce, brown sugar, garlic, chilli purée and peanut oil. Keep stirring until the sugar has dissolved.

Pour the soy sauce mixture over the chicken, turning the breasts over so that they are well coated. Cover and leave to marinate in a cool place for at least 2 hours.

To make the sauce, heat the rice vinegar and sugar gently in a small pan until the sugar dissolves. Simmer for 2 minutes, stirring regularly, then remove from the heat and stir in the ginger purée, red chilli and light soy sauce. Allow to cool.

Lift the chicken pieces from the marinade and barbecue them for 10–15 minutes or until cooked through, brushing regularly with any marinade left behind in the dish. Cut each chicken breast into 3 or 4 thick slices and serve with the sauce spooned over.

Ingredients

For the chicken:
4 skinless, boneless chicken breasts
2 tbsp light soy sauce
1 tbsp fish sauce
1 tsp granulated brown sugar
2 garlic cloves, peeled and crushed
1 tsp fresh chilli purée
1 tbsp peanut oil

For the sauce:
6 tbsp rice vinegar
2 tbsp raw sugar
½ tsp fresh ginger purée
1 red chilli, seeded and finely chopped
1 tbsp light soy sauce

Serves 4

RIGHT: In Bangkok, a street vendor barbecues quick, fresh dishes.

Chicken and pineapple with three-flavour sauce

Ingredients

For the three-flavour sauce:

2 tbsp peanut oil

2 cloves garlic, peeled and minced

1 tsp fresh ginger purée

1 medium red chilli, seeded and chopped

2 shallots, peeled and finely chopped

2 tbsp palm sugar (or dark muscovado sugar)

1 tsp tamarind paste

1 tbsp fish sauce

Juice of 3 limes

2 tbsp peanut oil

6 boneless chicken thighs, skinned and cut
  into bite-sized pieces

4 spring onions, trimmed and sliced

1 slice pineapple, cut into small pieces

150 ml (5 fl. oz) chicken stock

4 kaffir lime leaves, cut into wafer-thin strips

Serves 4

This dish is known in Thailand as gai tod saporot. It features a sauce that crops up in dishes all over the country, offering a balance of sour, sweet and salty flavours. Although it contains some chilli, the sauce is not particularly hot. If most diners prefer not to have the chilli content increased, lovers of hot food can add extra fire by adding nam prik (chilli sauce) as a condiment. Replace the chicken with raw shrimp if you prefer.

To make the sauce, heat the oil in a wok and fry the garlic, ginger, purée, chilli and shallots over a low heat for 3 minutes. Crumble in the sugar and cook until it caramelizes to a rich, red brown. Add the tamarind paste, fish sauce and lime juice and remove from the heat.

Heat the oil in a frying pan and stir-fry the chicken in two batches for 1–2 minutes over a brisk heat. Remove and set aside.

Add the spring onions and pineapple to the pan and stir-fry for 1 minute. Transfer the spring onions and pineapple to the three-flavour sauce in the wok, stir in the stock and bring to a simmer. Lower the heat, add the chicken and lime leaves and cook gently for 10 minutes.

Serve with noodles as well as a green vegetable, such as bok choy or mangetout peas.

Chicken pad thai

Chicken pad thai is one of Thailand's most popular and best-known noodle dishes. It requires a type of medium flat rice-stick noodle known as sen lek in Thai. A vegetarian version of this dish – minus the chicken and substituting vegetable for chicken stock – loses none of the taste, as it can easily be bulked out with additional tofu (bean curd). See page 164 for an alternative version of pad thai with shrimp.

Soak the noodles in hot water for 7–10 minutes, drain and set aside.

Mix the sauce ingredients together in a pan and boil until reduced to about two-thirds of a cup. Set aside to cool.

Drain the noodles. Heat the oil in a wok or frying pan until it just starts to smoke, and then stir-fry the chicken for 2–3 minutes. Add the chopped ginger, garlic and chilli, and stir-fry for 1 minute. Add the tofu and stir-fry for 1 minute, then break in the eggs. Stir-fry for 1 minute before adding the noodles and stock.

When the noodles are soft, add the remaining ingredients and the sauce, and stir-fry for 2 minutes. Garnish with the lemon and cucumber slices and the coriander leaves, and serve immediately.

Ingredients

For the noodles:

300 g (11 oz) dried medium flat rice-stick
  noodles
3 tbsp peanut or corn oil
175 g (6 oz) skinless, boneless chicken breast,
  finely sliced
1 cm (½ inch) fresh root ginger, finely chopped
2 cloves garlic, finely chopped
1 red bird's eye chilli, chopped
100 g (4 oz) tofu (also known as bean curd),
  diced
4 eggs
50 ml (2 fl. oz) chicken stock
3 tbsp sliced shallots
3 tbsp dried shrimp, chopped
75 g (3 oz) unsalted peanuts, chopped
4 spring onions, sliced
425 g (15 oz) bean sprouts
Fresh coriander leaves and slices of lemon and
  cucumber, to garnish

For the sauce:

225 ml (8 fl. oz) water
100 ml (4 fl. oz) tamarind juice
50 g (2 oz) sugar
1 tbsp light soy sauce

Serves 6

Fried rice noodles with chillies and vegetables

Using four red chillies, this is a fiery, hot dish. But it also has its more delicate flavours, particularly the lemongrass – a staple of many Thai dishes – which gives it a pleasant, tangy perfume.

Cook the noodles in lightly salted boiling water for 3 minutes. Drain and plunge into cold water, then drain again and reserve.

Heat the oil in a wok or large frying pan and stir-fry the lemongrass and ginger for 2 minutes. Discard the lemongrass and ginger, reserving the oil in the pan.

Add the onion, garlic, and chillies, and stir-fry for 2 minutes. Add the red pepper and cook for a further 2 minutes. Add the remaining vegetables and stir-fry for a further 2 minutes.

Finally add the reserved noodles and cashew nuts with the soy sauce, orange juice and honey. Stir-fry for 1 minute. Add the sesame oil and quickly stir-fry for a final 30 seconds. Serve immediately.

Ingredients

175 g (6 oz) dried medium rice-stick noodles

2 tbsp sunflower oil

2 lemongrass stalks, outer leaves removed and chopped

2.5-cm (1-in) piece fresh root ginger, peeled and grated

1 red onion, cut into thin wedges

2 garlic cloves, crushed

4 red bird's eye chillies, seeded and sliced

1 red pepper, seeded and cut into matchsticks

100 g (4 oz) carrot, very thinly sliced

100 g (4 oz) courgettes, trimmed and sliced

85 g (3 oz) mangetout peas, trimmed and cut diagonally in half

6 spring onions, trimmed and diagonally sliced

100 g (4 oz) cashew nuts

2 tbsp soy sauce

Juice of 1 orange

1 tsp clear honey

1 tbsp sesame oil

Serves 4

Spicy rice-stick noodles with chicken

Authentic Thai spicy noodles are very, very hot. If you don't think your taste buds can take it, simply reduce the number of green chillies that you use. However, if you feel like increasing the spiciness, you can add more green chillies, if you dare.

If you use fresh noodles, just rinse with warm water. Soak dried rice noodles in warm water for 2–5 minutes, or according to the instructions on the package. Rinse, and drain.

Heat 3 tablespoons of the oil in a wok or frying pan until very hot. Stir-fry the garlic and green chilli for 30 seconds, then add the chicken and fry for about 3 minutes more.

Add the green beans, mustard greens or spinach, and baby corn, stirring for 1–2 minutes. Add the remaining oil and the rice noodles, and stir. Then add the fish sauce, both soy sauces and sugar and stir well.

Garnish with the tomatoes, and serve immediately.

Ingredients

900 g (2 lb) fresh flat rice noodles or 275 g (10 oz) dried rice-stick noodles

5 tbsp vegetable oil

2 cloves garlic, finely chopped

4–6 small green chillies, chopped

225 g (8 oz) boneless chicken breasts, sliced into bite-sized pieces

100 g (4 oz) frozen green beans, halved

110 g (¼ lb) mustard greens or fresh spinach

16 canned or fresh baby corn, each cut diagonally into 3 pieces

4 tbsp fish sauce

3 tbsp dark soy sauce

2 tbsp light soy sauce

1 tbsp palm sugar (or dark muscovado sugar)

2 small tomatoes, halved, to garnish

Serves 4

Rice-stick noodles with pork and shrimp

Ingredients

275 g (10 oz) dried rice-stick noodles

5 tbsp vegetable oil

2 cloves garlic, finely chopped

3 shallots, chopped

225 g (8 oz) lean pork, sliced into small pieces

100 g (4 oz) peeled shrimp

4–6 small green chillies, chopped

275 g (10 oz) bean sprouts

3 stalks celery, cut diagonally into bite-sized
   pieces

2 eggs, beaten

2½ tbsp palm sugar (or dark muscovado
   sugar)

3½ tbsp tomato ketchup

6 tbsp fish sauce

15 ml (½ fl. oz) freshly squeezed lemon juice

Chopped coriander leaves, to garnish

Serves 4

This dish contains three of the main foundations of Thai flavouring: garlic, shallots and chillies. Thai garlic tends to be small compared to its Western counterpart, so if the cloves you have are on the large side, use just one.

Soak the rice-stick noodles in warm water for 2–5 minutes, or according to the instructions on the package. Rinse and drain.

Heat 3 tablespoons of the oil in a wok or frying pan, and stir-fry the garlic and shallots for 30 seconds. Add the pork and fry for about 3 minutes. Add the shrimp and green chillies, stirring for another minute, then add the bean sprouts and celery, and fry for another 2 minutes.

Make a well in the centre, then pour in the eggs and scramble quickly. Add the remaining oil and the rice-stick noodles, then stir. Add the sugar, tomato ketchup, fish sauce and lemon juice, and stir well.

Divide the noodles into four bowls, and garnish with chopped coriander.

Crisp fried rice vermicelli

*T*he thin, fried vermicelli rice noodles, known as sen mee in Thai, give this dish a delicious crisp texture. The noodles are sold dried in rolls and bound together in bundles. They need to be soaked briefly in cold water to soften them, but they must then be dried thoroughly before frying or they will spit dangerously when added to the hot oil. It is also important to heat the oil to the correct temperature or the vermicelli will be tough and chewy rather than crisp. If you don't have a cooking thermometer, place the handle of a wooden spoon in the hot oil; when bubbles form around it, the oil is ready.

Finely chop the chicken breast, cut the cooked pork into fine slices and set aside with the shrimp. Fry the shallots and garlic in hot oil in a wok; do not colour. Add the chicken and stir for 3–4 minutes, then stir in the pork and shrimp, turning continuously.

Add the tofu (bean curd) cubes and salted soybeans and cook for 2–3 minutes. Then add the beaten eggs little by little, stirring throughout and adding extra oil if necessary to the sauce.

At this stage stir in the vinegar, icing sugar and fish sauce. Toss in the pan for 1–2 minutes, then check the flavour. It should have a sweet, salty taste. Set aside.

In a large pan, heat oil to 180°C (375°F), or until a cube of bread dropped in turns golden in 60 seconds. Deep-fry the noodles for just a few seconds. This is best done in several stages in a frying basket or wok. The noodles will become puffy and crisp. Remove them from the fat. Drain and keep warm.

Just before serving, put half the sauce and a sprinkling of the chilli powder in a large wok or pan with half the noodles. Toss together without breaking up the noodles too much. Repeat the process with the remaining sauce, chilli and noodles.

Pile onto a large serving platter and garnish with chillies, coriander, garlic and lime or grapefruit zest. Arrange the spring onions all around the base.

Ingredients

For the sauce:
100 g (4 oz) raw, skinless, boneless chicken breast
50 g (2 oz) cooked pork
100 g (4 oz) cooked shrimp, shelled
Oil for frying
6 shallots, chopped
2 cloves garlic, crushed
1 square tofu (bean curd), yellow or white, cut into neat cubes
175 g (6 oz) canned salted soybeans
4 eggs, beaten
25 ml (1 fl. oz) cider or wine vinegar
1–2 tbsp icing sugar
Fish sauce to taste

For the noodles:
Fat for deep-frying
325 g (12 oz) rice vermicelli
¼ tsp chilli powder

For the garnish:
2–3 red chillies, seeded and finely sliced
Fresh coriander leaves
Pickled garlic or fried garlic flakes, chopped
Strip of lime or grapefruit zest
175 g (6 oz) spring onions

Serves 6–8

Crispy fried rice vermicelli with garlic, fish sauce and lime stir-fry sauce

Ingredients

For the garlic, fish sauce and lime
  stir-fry sauce:
1 tsp fresh garlic purée
Juice of 1 lime
1 tsp soft brown sugar
2 red chillies, seeded and finely chopped
3 tbsp fish sauce
1 tbsp rice vinegar

200 g (7 oz) rice vermicelli
Peanut oil for deep-frying
175 g (6 oz) lean pork, cut into small pieces
2 skinless, boneless chicken breasts, cut into
  small pieces
1 red pepper, seeded and chopped
100 g (4 oz) bean sprouts
2 large eggs, beaten
2 tbsp fresh coriander, to garnish

Serves 4

The three flavours of garlic, fish sauce and lime are the triumvirate of Thai cuisine. Here they combine to form the basis of a hot, salty, sweet and sour sauce for stir-frying pork, chicken and mixed vegetables. This dish is known as mee krob in Thailand. As with most stir-fries, you may vary the ingredients according to their availability. Shrimp, diced tofu, minced turkey and other vegetables, such as carrots, baby corn and spring onions, can also be used.

To make the sauce, simply mix the ingredients together, stirring until the sugar dissolves.

Snip the vermicelli into short lengths and soak briefly in cold water to soften. Dry thoroughly on paper towel.

In a wok heat the oil to 180°C (350°F), or until a cube of bread dropped into it turns golden in 60 seconds. Add the vermicelli a little at a time and fry until they are lightly golden and crisp. Drain on paper towel.

Pour off most of the oil from the wok, leaving about 2 tablespoons. Reheat, add the pork, and stir-fry for 2 minutes over high heat. Add the chicken and stir-fry for 3 minutes. Remove and set aside.

Add the red pepper, the bean sprouts and the mangetout peas and stir-fry for 3 minutes. Return the pork and chicken to the wok and add the sauce. Toss for 1 minute, then add the eggs and stir until they have set.

Add the noodles and herbs and toss together over the heat until well mixed. Garnish with fresh coriander and serve at once before the noodles have started to soften.

Chicken with peppers and bean-thread noodles

*B*ean-thread noodles – also known as cellophane noodles, glass noodles and woon sen in Thai – are a type of thin, dried transparent noodle made from mung beans. In this recipe they are accompanied by a tasty stir-fry that uses fresh kaffir lime leaves. If you have difficulty finding fresh ones, most supermarkets sell dried ones, or you could just leave them out.

Soak the bean-thread noodles in boiling water for 4 minutes, then drain and set aside until required.

Use a sharp knife to slice the peppers and carrots into thin strips, then grate the ginger, lemongrass and garlic.

Cut the chicken into strips. Heat a wok until hot then add the oil. Heat for 30 seconds, then stir-fry the chilli, lime leaves, ginger, lemongrass and garlic for 1 minute. Add the chicken strips and continue to stir-fry for 3 minutes, or until browned.

Add the pepper and carrot and stir-fry for 4 minutes. Add the noodles and stir-fry for 2 minutes. Pour in the soy sauce and fish sauce and stir-fry for another 2 minutes, or until the chicken is completely cooked through. Sprinkle with the chopped coriander and serve immediately.

Ingredients
225 g (8 oz) bean-thread noodles
1 red pepper, seeded
1 yellow pepper, seeded
1 green pepper. seeded
2 carrots
5-cm (2-in) piece fresh root ginger
2 lemongrass stalks, outer leaves discarded
2–4 cloves garlic
2 x 150-g (5-oz) skinless, boneless chicken breasts
2 tbsp groundnut oil
1–2 Thai chillies (see page 20), seeded and chopped
2 kaffir lime leaves
2 tbsp light soy sauce
1 tbsp fish sauce
2 tbsp chopped coriander, to garnish

Serves 4

Fried bean-thread noodles with tofu

Ingredients

For the noodles:

225 g (8 oz) bean-thread noodles

4 tbsp vegetable oil

275 g (10 oz) tofu (bean curd), diced

3 cloves garlic, finely chopped

450 g (1 lb) bean sprouts

100 g (4 oz) frozen green beans, halved

2 spring onions, chopped

2 tbsp roast peanuts, crushed

2 tbsp dried shrimp, chopped

3–5 small green chillies, chopped

2½ tbsp palm sugar (or dark muscovado sugar)

6 tbsp fish sauce

100 ml (4 fl. oz) freshly squeezed lemon juice

For the garnish:

2 tbsp crisp onions

Coriander leaves

1 medium red chilli, sliced

Lime slices

Serves 4

Tofu, or bean curd, is a favourite constituent of Thai cooking. Note that it is always best to use all of your tofu in one go as it quickly deteriorates, even if refrigerated.

Soak the bean-thread noodles in boiling water for 5 minutes. Rinse under cold water, and drain. Heat half the oil in a wok or frying pan, and fry the tofu until golden brown. Drain on paper towel.

Add the remaining oil to the wok, then fry the garlic for about 30 seconds. Add the bean sprouts, green beans and spring onions, and stir well.

Stir in the bean-thread noodles, tofu, crushed peanuts, dried shrimp and green chilli. Season with the sugar, fish sauce and lemon juice, stirring again.

Transfer the noodles to four plates. Sprinkle with the crisp onions, coriander leaves and red chilli, and garnish with the lime slices. Serve at once.

LEFT: The Grand Palace in Bangkok is beautifully adorned with brightly coloured statues. It is the gem of Bangkok's impressive collection of temples and palaces.

Spicy egg noodles with beef and vegetables

*B**a mee, or Thai egg noodles, are the basis of this dish. They have a distinctive yellow colour in contrast to the more commonly used white rice noodles. The shrimp paste used in this recipe is highly pungent, but do not let the odour put you off. Wise Thai cooks make sure their kitchen is well ventilated while they are cooking.*

In a large saucepan, bring a quantity of water to a boil, add the egg noodles and cook for 4 minutes. Rinse under cold water and drain.

Heat the oil in a wok or frying pan, and stir-fry the red chillies, garlic and shrimp paste, if using. Add the beef and fry for 2–3 minutes or until cooked.

Add the onion, green chillies, bean sprouts and spinach stirring in each ingredient well. Season to taste with the salt and pepper.

Add the noodles, sprinkle over both soy sauces and mix well. Divide the noodles among four plates and garnish with coriander leaves and lime wedges. Serve immediately.

Ingredients
275 g (10 oz) dried, medium egg noodles
3 tbsp vegetable oil
2–3 small dried red chillies, soaked in hot
    water, then ground
2 cloves garlic, finely chopped
1 tsp dried shrimp paste (optional)
275 g (10 oz) round steak, thinly sliced
1 medium onion, thinly sliced
2 green chillies, chopped
200 g (7 oz) bean sprouts
100 g (4 oz) fresh spinach
Salt and black pepper, freshly ground
3 tbsp dark soy sauce and light soy sauce
Coriander leaves
4 lime wedges

Serves 4

Egg noodles with tofu and vegetables

... *hip of flavours that is classic in Thai cooking.* ... *are served with a distinctive, aromatic sauce.*

Cook the noodles in a pan of boiling water for 4 minutes, then drain. Blanch the peas in another pan of boiling water for 2 minutes before draining.

Heat the oil in a wok or frying pan, add the garlic, shallots and chillies, and stir-fry for 2 minutes. Add the tofu and stir-fry for 2 minutes more.

Add the bean sprouts and carrot and stir-fry for 2 minutes. Add the noodles, fish sauce, lime juice and sugar. Stir-fry over a high heat for 2–3 minutes. Before serving, sprinkle the coriander and peanuts over the noodles and garnish with lime wedges.

Ingredients
275 g (10 oz) dried medium egg noodles
100 g (4 oz) sugar snap peas, cut into halves
2 tbsp sunflower oil
2 cloves garlic, minced
2 shallots, sliced
3 small green chillies, chopped
275 g (10 oz) firm tofu, diced into 1-cm (½-in) cubes
100 g (4 oz) bean sprouts, rinsed
1 carrot, shredded
2 tbsp fish sauce
2 tbsp fresh lime juice
1 tbsp brown sugar
3 tbsp chopped fresh coriander
2 tbsp roasted peanuts, chopped
4 lime wedges, to garnish

Serves 4

Mango sorbet

A water ice made with ripe mangoes, this sorbet needs beating every hour until it is frozen to break up the large ice crystals, but it should still retain an icy, grainy texture. You can subsitute any really ripe soft fruit for the mango.

Make a syrup by bringing the water and sugar to the boil, stirring to help dissolve the sugar. Simmer for a few minutes, then remove from the heat and allow to cool.

Remove the mangoes' skin and rind, cut into pieces and feed through an electric strainer to create a thick purée. Then mix the purée with the syrup and lemon juice.

If you are using an ice cream machine, follow the manufacturer's instructions, adding the egg white for the last 5 minutes of the churning.

If you do not have an ice cream machine, add the egg whites to the mango purée, then turn into a shallow plastic container. Open-freeze the sorbet, removing from the freezer every hour and beating to break up the ice crystals.

When almost frozen, but still liquid in the centre, tip the mixture into a mixing bowl and beat until free of ice crystals.

Before serving, place the container in the refrigerator for 1 hour to soften the sorbet and make it easier to scoop out.

Ingredients

225 ml (8 fl. oz) water

80 g (3¼ oz) caster sugar

2 large ripe mangoes, peeled, pitted and cubed

Juice of 1 lemon

1 large egg white, lightly beaten

Serves 4

Lemongrass and lime mousse

Ingredients

2 lemongrass stalks, tough outer layers
   removed

50 ml (2 fl. oz) water

2 eggs, separated

90 g (3½ oz) caster sugar

Grated zest of 1 lime, plus extra to decorate

Juice of 1½ limes

300 ml (10 fl. oz) double cream

15 g (½ oz) powdered gelatine

Serves 4

*T*his mousse has a wonderfully delicate flavour and provides a light, clean finish to a meal.

Using a rolling pin, thoroughly crush the lemongrass to release its flavour. Place in a saucepan, cover with water and simmer for 10 minutes. Allow to cool in the pan.

Meanwhile, using a food mixer, whisk the egg yolk with the sugar on the fastest speed setting until you have a thick, pale mixture. Add the lime zest, lime juice and cream and briefly whisk again.

When cool, remove the lemongrass from the pan and discard. Reheat until almost boiling, then sprinkle the gelatine over the liquid, remove from the heat and stir until the gelatine has dissolved completely. Allow to cool slightly and then, with the mixer running at medium speed, slowly pour the gelatine onto the egg mixture until thoroughly combined. Transfer to another bowl and set aside.

Wash the whisk and mixing bowl thoroughly before whisking the egg whites until firm. Add to the mixture in the reserved bowl and fold in until just combined.

Pour into four individual serving dishes and refrigerate for 1–2 hours. Sprinkle with lime zest to serve.

LEFT: The bold beauty of Canna Lilies are a common sight in Thailand. According to Thai mythology, Canna Lilies are guarded by deities who bless them with peace and harmony.

CHAPTER TWO

Northern Thailand

This is a mountainous region dotted with many thick forests. The soils here are extremely fertile, producing a wide range of vegetables which find their way into many local dishes. Far from the coast, the people here enjoy little fresh seafood. Pork, chicken and beef are the main sources of protein, often cooked in mild curry sauces that bear the culinary imprint of Burma to the north. Indian ingredients, such as ginger, turmeric and tamarind, are also popular. Coconut is used less widely than in the tropical south. Instead, tomatoes, which elsewhere feature mainly as a salad vegetable, form the basis of many sauces. Almost all meals are accompanied by sticky rice, which is rolled into balls and dipped into sauces using the fingers.

LEFT: Despite the distance from the coast, dishes like fishcakes are a seafood favourite in Chiang Mai.

Sticky rice

*I*n northern and northeastern Thailand almost all meals are accompanied by a special type of rice known as sticky or 'glutinous' rice. True to its name, the rice's high starch content makes the grains stick together when cooked. Thai people use their fingers to roll the rice into balls and dip it into sauces. Note that for the best results, the rice grains need first to be soaked in water for several hours.

Ingredients
225 g (8 oz) sticky rice

Serves 4

Put the sticky rice in a bowl and pour over cold water to cover by 5 cm (2 in). Leave the rice to soak for at least 4 hours or overnight.

Rinse the rice 3 times in lukewarm water and drain very well.

Transfer the rice to a steamer lined with muslin. Be careful to spread the grains out.

Steam for 20–25 minutes until the rice is tender. Do not let the boiling water touch the bottom of the rice.

The rice should be taken off the heat and allowed to rest for about 10 minutes before it is served.

Spicy meat and tomato dip

Ingredients

6 dried red chillies, chopped

3 tbsp chopped shallots

1 tbsp sliced lemongrass

1 tbsp chopped garlic

2 tsp shrimp paste

2 tsp salt

2 tbsp peanut or corn oil

100 g (4 oz) ground pork

8 cherry tomatoes, diced

100 ml (4 fl. oz) water

Lemon juice, to taste

Fish sauce, to taste (optional)

Sugar, to taste (optional)

25 g (1 oz) chopped coriander, to garnish

50 g (2 oz) crisp pork rinds, to serve

Serves 4–6

This relatively mild dip, known as nam prik ong in Thai, is heavily influenced by the cooking of neighbouring Burma. In typical northern Thai fashion, guests eat from the bowl in which it is served, scooping it up with the accompanying pork rinds, vegetables or sticky rice.

Pound the chillies, shallots, lemongrass, garlic, shrimp paste and salt together with a pestle and mortar or in a food mixer to produce a smooth paste.

Heat the oil in a wok or frying pan and add the chilli mixture, pork and tomatoes. Cook for about 15 minutes, or until the sauce has thickened. Add the water and cook again for 10 minutes until thick.

Adjust the seasoning to taste with lemon juice, and the fish sauce or sugar. Garnish with the coriander.

Serve accompanied by raw or slightly cooked vegetables, sticky rice, and if you can buy them, crisp pork rinds.

Northern Thai soup

*I*n the landlocked north, dried shrimp, sold in markets throughout the region, is often used instead of fresh varieties. The shrimp, fish sauce and tamarind juice give this dish a salty, tart taste.

Soak the shrimp in cold water for 5 minutes. Drain and leave to dry on a paper towel.

Boil the water in a saucepan, add the chicken and cook for 7–10 minutes until well cooked. Remove and cut across into thin slices.

Using the same cooking water, add the pork, preserved cabbage, onion and fish sauce. Simmer and then add the rest of the ingredients.

Boil again before pouring into bowls. Serve accompanied by sticky rice (see page 86).

Ingredients
475 ml (16 fl. oz) water
175 g (6 oz) skinless, boneless chicken breasts
275 g (10 oz) ground pork
1 tbsp preserved cabbage
100 g (4 oz) onion, sliced
2 tbsp fish sauce
15 g (½ oz) dried large shrimp
15 g (½ oz) spinach leaf
2 tbsp tamarind juice

Serves 4–6

Raw beef salad

The peoples of both northern and northeastern Thailand have a special fondness for raw meat dishes. This recipe is extremely easy and quick to prepare. For the best results, use high-quality beef and chop it up at the last minute.

Finely chop the beef sirloin using a sharp knife. Cut the beef liver into thin slices. Transfer all the chopped meat to a mixing bowl.

Add the remaining ingredients – the beef blood, mint leaves, spring onions, lime juice, fish sauce and chilli powder – to the mixing bowl. Using your fingers, carefully mix the ingredients together.

Transfer the salad out onto serving plates, and serve accompanied by raw swamp cabbage, raw cabbage wedges, fresh basil, onion rings and sticky rice (see page 86).

Ingredients

200 g (7 oz) very fresh lean beef sirloin
50 g (2 oz) beef liver
50 ml (2 fl. oz) very fresh beef blood
25 g (1 oz) mint leaves
3 tbsp finely sliced spring onion
3 tbsp lime or lemon juice
½ tbsp fish sauce
1½ tsp chilli powder
1 red onion, chopped into rings

Serves 6

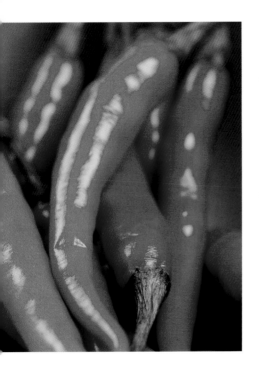

Northern Thai chicken curry with red chillies

A spicy chicken curry with no curry powder – instead northern Thai cooks use chopped red chillies to add fire to this dish. The chicken is cooked with its skin and bones to add extra flavour.

Heat the oil in a pan, add the chilli paste and fry over a medium heat for 1 minute. Add the chicken pieces, fry until they begin to brown, then add the water and the remaining ingredients.

Simmer until the chicken is tender and the curry reduced to about half its original volume. This should take around 20 minutes.

Serve accompanied by rice.

Ingredients
Peanut or corn oil, for frying
50 g (2 oz) chilli paste (see page 51)
450 g (1 lb) chicken (with skin and bone), cut
   into small pieces through the bones
1.5 litres (2½ pints) water
4 kaffir lime leaves, quartered
2 stalks of lemongrass, halved
1 tbsp fish sauce

Serves 4–6

Northern Thai pork curry

*T*his dish originally came from across the Burmese border, as shown by the use of tamarind and turmeric. The palm sugar adds a hint of sweetness, which nicely offsets the tart flavour of this curry.

Pound the lemongrass, galangal, shrimp paste and chillies to a smooth paste with a pestle and mortar or blend in a food mixer, then mix with the pork.

Transfer the paste to a saucepan with the water, turmeric and soy sauce. Bring to a boil and simmer until tender, which should take about 15 minutes, then add the rest of the ingredients. Boil again for 5–8 minutes, then remove from the heat.

Taste and season with fish sauce if wished.

Ingredients

4 stalks lemongrass, chopped
1 tbsp chopped galangal
1 tbsp shrimp paste
4 dried red chillies, chopped
1 kg (2¼ lb) pork belly, cut into 1-cm (½-in) thick strips
650 ml (1¼ pints) cold water
1 tbsp turmeric
1 tsp soy sauce
10 shallots, sliced
50 g (2 oz) palm sugar (or dark muscovado sugar)
50 g (2 oz) fresh root ginger, chopped and pounded
50 ml (2 fl. oz) tamarind juice
2 tbsp garlic, chopped
½ tbsp soybeans
Fish sauce, to taste (optional)

Serves 6

Curried noodles

Ingredients

1.5 litres (2½ pints) thin coconut milk
4 tbsp red chilli paste (see page 51)
300 g (11 oz) skinless, boneless chicken
  breasts, cut lengthways into 1-cm (½-in)
  thick slices
1 tbsp light soy sauce
1 tbsp dark soy sauce
2 tsp salt
200 g (7 oz) dried or 400 g (14 oz) fresh egg
  noodles
Peanut or corn oil, for frying

Serves 4–6

This is a favourite lunch in Chiang Mai and other towns in northern Thailand. The curry ingredients reveal its Indian antecedents, but khao soi, as it is known, has arrived via Burma, in particular from Shan State. The crispy noodles are added at the last minute to stop them from going soggy, while the various condiments give each diner some control over the dish's flavour.

Heat 300 ml (½ pint) of the coconut milk in a frying pan or wok, add the chilli paste and fry for 2 minutes, then add the chicken and soy sauces. Stir-fry for 3 minutes, then add the remaining coconut milk and bring to a boil for 3 minutes. Add the salt and remove from the heat.

Fry 100 g (4 oz) of the noodles in hot oil until crisp. Remove and drain well. Boil the remaining noodles in water until firm but tender, then drain.

Transfer the boiled noodles to individual serving bowls and pour the chicken mixture on top. Garnish with the fried noodles.

Serve accompanied by bowls of diced shallots, pickled cabbage and chilli powder.

Chiang Mai noodles with chicken

*T*his Thai speciality is also known as khao soi, and is originally *from the Chiang Mai area in the northwestern part of Thailand. Ensure you use fresh egg noodles – or soak dried noodles for 20 minutes before you start cooking.*

Heat the peanut oil in a wok. Add the red curry paste and the chilli powder. Cook gently for 2–3 minutes.

Add 150 ml (5 fl. oz) coconut milk and the chicken. Continue to stir-fry for 2–3 minutes.

Turn the heat down and add chicken stock, fish sauce and the remaining coconut milk. While the chicken is cooking, boil the noodles and drain. Transfer the noodles to a large bowl. When the chicken is cooked pour over the noodles.

Garnish with chopped shallots, spring onions and coriander. Serve with lime wedges.

Ingredients

1 tbsp peanut oil
2 tbsp red curry paste (see page 156)
2 tbsp chilli powder
650 ml (1¼ pints) coconut milk
275 g (10 oz) chicken, chopped
650 ml (1¼ pints) chicken stock
1 tbsp fish sauce
225 g (8 oz) egg noodles
100 g (4 oz) shallots, chopped
Few sprigs of coriander, to garnish
2 spring onions, chopped, to garnish
1 lime, cut in wedges, to serve

Serves 4

Chiang Mai sausages

Ingredients

1 tbsp fish sauce

2 cloves garlic

2 tbsp coriander leaves

1 tbsp lemongrass purée

1 tbsp galangal (or ginger) purée

2 tbsp red curry paste (see page 156)

2 red chillies, seeded and roughly chopped

4 kaffir lime leaves

450 g (1 lb) ground pork

75-cm (30-in) sausage casing

Sprig of Thai basil

Makes 6

*S*ai ua is the name given to the spicy sausages from Chiang Mai that are sold on street stalls throughout the city. They come in a variety of shapes and sizes, from small bite-sized balls to long spirals filled with enough meat to feed an entire family.

Place the fish sauce, garlic, coriander leaves, lemongrass and galangal purée, curry paste, chillies and lime leaves in a pestle and mortar, or food mixer, and blend to a fine paste.

Place the pork in a mixing bowl. Add the paste and thoroughly mix together. Leave to marinate in the fridge for at least 2 hours or overnight.

Use your fingers to push the mixture into the sausage casing. Make each sausage around 10 cm (4 in) long and tie off the ends.

Fry or grill the sausages and serve with sticky rice (see page 86) and a sprig of Thai basil.

LEFT: Doi Suthep temple in Chiang Mai. Doi Suthep mountain is one of the most revered religious destinations in Thailand.

Flat breads

Bread is uncharacteristic of Thai cooking. This recipe found its way into the north of the country from India, via Burma. These rotis are mainly eaten as dessert snacks rather than as part of a main meal.

Mix all the ingredients, except for the oil, together well in a bowl – if the mixture is too wet to shape, add a little more flour. Shape the dough into bite-sized balls and flatten them into 10-cm (4-in) circles by throwing them onto a lightly floured table surface – be careful to throw them quite horizontal.

Heat just enough oil to cover the bottom of a frying pan. Working in batches, place the flattened dough balls in the pan and cook over medium heat for about 3–4 minutes on each side, until lightly browned. Drain on paper towel and repeat, until all the dough balls are cooked.

Three delicious ways of serving the flat breads are: to place an egg on top of each browned roti, flipping it over to cook the egg and rolling it up to eat (perhaps with coffee); sprinkle them with sugar and condensed milk; or spread them with butter.

Ingredients

175 g (6 oz) plain flour
50 ml (2 fl. oz) water
1 tbsp butter, softened
1 egg
¼ tsp salt
Peanut or corn oil, for frying

Makes 7–8

Sticky rice with mangoes

Ingredients
400 g (14 oz) sticky rice (see page 86)
400 ml (14 fl. oz) thin coconut milk
50 g (2 oz) sugar
½ tsp salt
½ tsp cornflour
2 ripe mangoes, peeled and sliced
Mint leaves, to decorate

Serves 6

A simple but always successful dessert, this works because of the delicious contrast between the sticky, tangy rice and the sweet, juicy, yellow Thai mango.

Soak the rice in water for 4 hours, rinse well three times in lukewarm water and drain very well. Transfer the drained rice to a steamer lined with muslin. Be careful to spread the grains out. Cover and steam for about 25–30 minutes until fairly soft.

Mix 350 ml (12 fl. oz) of the coconut milk with the sugar and half of the salt. Stir in the rice and mix well.

Mix the remaining coconut milk with the remaining salt and the cornflour together in a small saucepan, bring to a boil, simmer for 2 minutes and cool.

Place the sticky rice on serving plates, spoon the coconut sauce over the top and arrange the mango slices around the edges. Decorate with the mint leaves.

CHAPTER THREE

Northeastern Thailand

Of all the people in Thailand, those of the northeast, or I-san region, enjoy perhaps the most varied and interesting diet. A combination of poor soil and frequent floods has led the locals to acquire tastes for some very unusual ingredients. Red ant salad, fried grasshoppers and lizard curry are all dishes that can be enjoyed by curious visitors. It is probably this 'needs-must' approach to cooking that accounts for the strength of the local sauces. Here people like their food spicy, as shown in two of the region's most famous dishes: larb, a strong, sour salad, traditionally made with raw meat and blood; and som-tam, an extremely spicy green papaya salad. As in northern Thailand, most meals are accompanied by sticky rice.

LEFT: A candle ceremony in Uborachathani, northeastern Thailand.

Green papaya salad with lemongrass, coriander and ginger dressing

Salads are an important part of Thai cuisine, particularly in the northeast where green papaya salads are extremely popular. A 'green' papaya is one that is slightly under-ripe so that the salad is not too sweet or soft. Only the freshest ingredients should be used, which is why in Thailand most people shop early at their local market before the sun has had a chance to wilt the delicate produce. The papaya should be prepared just before serving so that it does not lose its firm texture. This particular recipe, which features pork and mango, is known as yam mamuang.

To make the dressing, simply mix all the ingredients together in a bowl.

Heat the oil in a frying pan, add the shallot and fry for 5 minutes. Add the garlic, pork and ground coriander and stir over a fairly high heat for a couple of minutes until the pork starts to brown. Add the soy sauce and cook, stirring occasionally, until the sauce has been absorbed by the meat and the pork is quite dry. Remove from the heat and set aside.

Using a pestle and mortar, pound the papaya with 2 tablespoons of the dressing or blend to a coarse purée in a food processor. Spoon into a serving dish, top with the warm pork, mango and tomatoes, and pour over the remaining dressing. Serve garnished with fresh coriander.

Ingredients

For the dressing:
½ tsp fresh lemongrass purée
1 tsp fresh ginger purée
1 tbsp chopped fresh coriander
2 tbsp fish sauce
1 tbsp chopped mint
Juice of 2 limes
1 tsp soft light brown sugar
2 red chillies, seeded and finely chopped

2 tbsp peanut oil
1 shallot, peeled and finely chopped
1 garlic clove, peeled and minced
250 g (9 oz) finely ground pork
1 tsp ground coriander
2 tbsp light soy sauce
250 g (9 oz) unripe green papaya, seeded, peeled and cut into matchsticks
1 mango, peeled and chopped
4 cherry tomatoes, halved or quartered
Fresh coriander, to garnish

Serves 4

Spicy green papaya and vegetable salad

Ingredients

1 medium green papaya, peeled and
    quartered, seeds removed

½ cucumber, cut in half lengthways, seeds
    removed

2 carrots, peeled

2 tbsp chopped unsalted and roasted peanuts

2 garlic cloves, finely chopped

3–5 green chillies, to taste

1 tbsp sugar

1½ tbsp lime juice

1 tbsp fish sauce

15 cooked shrimp (optional)

4 fine green beans, topped, tailed and
    chopped into 2.5-cm (1-in) pieces

4 cherry tomatoes, halved

1 tbsp finely chopped flat-leaf parsley

3 mint leaves, finely chopped

Serves 2

*T*his salad, known as som tam, is bursting with invigorating flavours and fragrances. If you can't find green, under-ripe papaya (the inside will be white), leave the papaya out altogether and use extra cucumber (seeds removed) and carrot (peeled), or a mixture of both, instead. A ripe papaya will simply turn to mush used in this recipe.

First, grate the papaya and vegetables, then cover and set aside.

Prepare the dressing. In a food mixer, blend half the peanuts, the garlic and the chillies together for about 3 minutes. Then, with the mixer set on a slow speed, add the remaining ingredients, ending with the grated vegetables. Mix everything together until thoroughly combined.

Serve on a large platter with the remaining peanuts sprinkled over the top.

Crab, pomelo and rice noodle salad

A mixture of seafood, green papaya and pomelos, this salad takes just 15 minutes to prepare and makes a light but satisfying lunch.

Cook the rice noodles according to the package instructions and drain.

Mix together the lime juice, red chilli, fish sauce and sugar, stirring until the sugar dissolves. Toss with the warm noodles and set them aside to cool.

Cut the cucumber into long strips using a vegetable peeler. Peel the pomelo, pull away the pith and break the flesh into bite-sized segments.

Add the cucumber, pomelo, grated green papaya and crab claws to the noodles and toss lightly together.

Transfer to a serving dish and serve with lime wedges to squeeze over the salad.

Ingredients

250 g (9 oz) dried medium rice-stick noodles
Juice of 2 limes
1 red chilli, seeded and very thinly
  sliced
2 tbsp fish sauce
1 tsp caster sugar
½ cucumber
1 pomelo
150 g (5 oz) green papaya, peeled and grated
12 crab claws
Lime wedges, to serve

Serves 4

Fried fish spicy salad

Ingredients

550 g (1¼ lb) fillets of firm, white fish, such as
    cod or haddock

Peanut or corn oil, for deep-frying

1 green under-ripe mango, cut into
    matchsticks

50 g (2 oz) unsalted roasted peanuts

7 fresh small green chillies, chopped

3 tbsp shallots, sliced

3 tbsp fish sauce

2 tbsp coriander leaves and stems, cut into
    2.5-cm (1-in) pieces, to garnish

Serves 4–6

*T*his crisp salad is often served as a snack to accompany drinks –
an important and distinct category of dish in Thailand, where
drinking tends to be separated from the eating of the main meal.

Steam the fish for 15 minutes until well cooked. Remove any skin or bones and chop into slices.

Heat the oil in a wok or pan to 180°C (350°F), or until a cube of bread dropped in turns golden in 60 seconds. Sprinkle in the chopped fish and fry until light brown and crispy, which should take around 3–5 minutes. Remove with a slotted spoon or strainer and drain well.

Mix all the remaining ingredients except the coriander with the fish. Transfer the salad to serving plates, garnish with the coriander and serve accompanied by sticky rice or bean sprout salad.

Grilled beef salad with fish sauce, herb and lime dressing

This spicy grilled beef salad, known as yum nua, is enlivened by the addition of a hot and sour dressing. Because the beef in yum nua is only lightly cooked, it must be as tender as possible, so sirloin, rump and fillet steak are the best cuts to use. Trim any fat from the steak before grilling, and after grilling allow it to stand for 10 minutes so it is easier to carve into very thin slices. A cast-iron ridged grill pan is recommended because it can be heated to a sufficiently high temperature to seal the meat and ensure that it stays tender, but a conventional grill could be used as well.

To make the dressing, place the ingredients in a covered container and shake well, or whisk together in a bowl until combined and the sugar has dissolved.

Brush the steak with the oil and cook in a grill pan over a high heat until well-browned but still pink in the centre. Alternatively, grill the meat under high heat and set aside for 10 minutes, reserving any juices that have come out.

Arrange the lettuce, rocket, onion, tomato slices, spring onions and cucumber on a serving dish. With a sharp knife, slice the steak as thinly as possible and mix the slices in with the salad leaves and vegetables. Whisk any meat juices into the dressing and spoon this over the salad.

Toss lightly and serve sprinkled with the sliced chilli.

Ingredients

For the dressing:
2 tbsp fish sauce
2 cloves garlic, peeled and minced
1 tbsp rice vinegar
Juice of 1 lime
1 tsp soft brown sugar
2 tbsp chopped fresh coriander
2 tbsp chopped mint

For the salad:
450 g (1 lb) fillet or thick sirloin steak in one piece
2 tbsp peanut oil
90 g (3½ oz) mixed lettuce and rocket leaves
1 small onion, peeled and finely sliced
2 spring onions, sliced
2 tomatoes, cut into thin wedges
½ cucumber, cut into thin strips
1 red chilli, seeded and sliced, to garnish

Serves 6

Spiced ground chicken

One of the special characteristics of this northeastern meat dish is the addition of uncooked sticky rice, which is first roasted (either in an oven or in a dry wok) until golden and then pounded in a mortar. It adds a slightly nutty flavour and gives the dish more body.

Cook the chicken in a nonstick frying pan over a low heat for 10 minutes – do not add water or oil. When cooked, transfer to a bowl and mix well with all the remaining ingredients, except the mint.

Check the seasoning and add more lemon juice, fish sauce or chilli as necessary. Sprinkle the mint over the top to garnish.

Serve accompanied by raw cabbage leaves, spring onions and raw string beans.

Ingredients

450 g (1 lb) finely ground chicken

50 g (2 oz) shallots, sliced

Coriander leaves, chopped

4 tbsp sticky rice, roasted for 8–10 minutes until brown then pounded finely

4 tbsp lemon juice, or to taste

3 tbsp fish sauce, or to taste

1 tbsp chopped dried red chilli, or to taste

½ tsp sugar

Fresh mint leaves, to garnish

Raw cabbage leaves, spring onion and raw string beans, to serve

Serves 6

Wild boar country curry

Wild boar is not strictly necessary (and in any case, tends to be bred rather than hunted in Thailand these days). You can replace it with pork or venison. The flavour of krachai ginger adds an authentic Thai aroma.

Heat the oil in a wok or frying pan and fry the chilli paste for 3 minutes. Add the meat and stir-fry for 2 minutes; then add the water and bamboo shoots and cook until the shoots are tender, about 3–5 minutes.

Add the aubergines, string beans, krachai or ginger, chillies, fish sauce and lime leaves. Boil for 3 minutes more and then remove from the heat. Stir in the basil and serve.

Serve accompanied by pickled garlic, salted eggs and sticky rice (see page 86).

Ingredients

50 g (2 oz) chilli paste (see page 51)

4 tbsp peanut or corn oil

225 g (8 oz) boar, pork, or venison loin, cut into 2.5 x 2 x 0.5-cm (1 x ¾ x ¼-in) slices

1 litre (2 pints) water

200 g (7 oz) bamboo shoots, diced

150 g (5 oz) small white aubergines

115 g (4½ oz) string beans

50 g (2 oz) krachai or 25 g (1 oz) fresh root ginger, peeled and sliced lengthways

3 fresh red chillies, quartered

2 tbsp fish sauce

3 kaffir lime leaves, torn into small pieces

50 g (2 oz) basil leaves

Serves 4

Spicy pork curry

Juice of 2 limes

Peanut oil, for frying

4 green chillies, seeded and roughly chopped

2 shallots, thinly sliced

2 tbsp roughly chopped coriander leaves

2 tbsp fish sauce

75 g (3 oz) unsalted, roasted peanuts, roughly chopped

Sprigs of Thai basil, to garnish

Serves 4

Known as larb, this is the archetypal dish of northeast Thailand, where it is usually made with raw meat. However, as this recipe uses pork, for safety's sake it's important to make sure that the meat is thoroughly cooked. Serve with sticky rice (see page 86) and a spicy green papaya salad (see page 109).

Place the pork in a mixing bowl and squeeze over three-quarters of the lime juice. Use your hands to mix the juice with the pork. Place in the fridge to marinate for 20 minutes.

Heat the oil in a frying pan. Add the pork mixture and chillies and fry until thoroughly cooked, which should take around 5–6 minutes.

Transfer the mixture to a clean mixing bowl. Add the shallots, coriander, fish sauce, the remaining lime juice and all but a handful of peanuts. Use a wooden spoon to mix all the ingredients together.

Garnish with the remaining peanuts and the Thai basil. Serve immediately.

Spicy noodle salad with shrimp

*K*nown as *yam woonsen*, this is a filling and flavourful salad. The fish sauce is an essential flavour-enhancing ingredient. Prepare the dish at least 30 minutes before serving so the full, sweet, hot flavour has time to mature.

Soak the noodles in warm water for 5 minutes or according to the instructions on the package. Rinse under cold water and drain.

In a bowl, combine in the fish sauce, lemon juice and sugar, add the shrimps and marinate for 5 minutes. Meanwhile, mix together the dressing ingredients in a bowl.

Heat the sunflower oil in a frying pan and stir-fry the shrimp until cooked.

Put the pepper, celery, carrot, spring onions and noodles in a bowl and mix together. Place a lettuce leaf on each plate and spoon in the noodle mixture. Top with the shrimp, sprinkle with the coriander and serve with the dressing.

Ingredients
200 g (7 oz) bean thread noodles
16 large fresh shrimps, shelled and deveined
1 tsp fish sauce
2 tsp freshly squeezed lemon juice
1 tsp soft brown sugar
1 tbsp sunflower oil
1 small red pepper, finely chopped
2 sticks celery, finely sliced
100 g (4 oz) carrots, cut into matchsticks
2 spring onions, chopped
4 iceberg lettuce leaves
Fresh coriander, to garnish

For the dressing:
2 shallots, chopped fine
1 dry red chilli, crushed
3 small green chillies, chopped
4 tbsp fish sauce
100 ml (4 fl. oz) freshly squeezed lemon juice
4½ tbsp granulated sugar
1 tbsp sunflower oil

Serves 4

Coconut sticky rice with mango, papaya and lime

Ingredients

200 g (7 oz) sticky rice (see page 86)

175 ml (6 fl. oz) coconut milk

1 mango, peeled and chopped

½ papaya, peeled, seeded and chopped

Juice of 2 limes

Serves 4

With coconut, mangoes and papaya all competing for attention, this can be a very sweet dessert, although the lime adds a welcome note of tartness.

Put the sticky rice in a bowl and pour over cold water to cover by 5 cm (2 in). Leave the rice to soak for several hours or overnight.

Drain the rice and transfer to a steamer lined with muslin, spreading the grains out.

Steam for 20–25 minutes until the rice is tender. Warm the coconut milk and mix with the rice.

Leave the rice to stand for 15 minutes before serving with the mango and papaya, squeezing the lime juice over the fruit.

Fruit salad with lime and papaya sauce

Seductively aromatic when ripe, papayas are highly prized in northeastern Thai cooking, not just for their flavour but also for their healing properties. An open wound is said to heal more quickly after the application of a papaya poultice.

Prepare the fruit as necessary and cut into bite-sized pieces.

To make the sauce, roughly chop the papaya flesh and place in a food processor with three-quarters of the lime zest and all the juice. Add the tropical fruit juice and reduce to a smooth purée, adjusting the amount of juice, if necessary, according to the size of the papaya.

Serve the sauce with the fruit salad and the remaining lime zest scattered over. Decorate each serving with a kaffir lime leaf.

Ingredients

For the fruit salad:
700 g (1½ lb) tropical fruits, such as mango, pineapple, rambutan, longan

For the sauce:
1 ripe medium-sized papaya, peeled and seeded
Finely grated zest and juice of 2 limes
175 ml (6 fl. oz) tropical fruit juice
Kaffir lime leaves, to decorate

Serves 4

Central Thailand

- Chai Nat Province
- Lop Buri Province
- Sing Bori Province
- Ang Thong Province
- Nakhon Nayok Province
- Kanchanaburi Province
- Suphan Buri Province
- Saraburi Province
- Prachin Buri Province
- Sa Kaeo Province
- Samut Songkhram Province
- Ratchaburi Province
- Chachoengsao Province
- Chon Buri Province
- Phetchaburi Province
- Rayong Province
- Chanthaburi Province
- Prachuap Khiri Khan Province
- Samut Prakan Province
- Bangkok Metropolis Province
- Pathum Thani Province
- Phra Nakhon Si Ayutthaya Province
- Nonthaburi Province
- Samut Sakhon Province
- Nakhon Pathom Province
- Trat Province

The Thai heartland, comprising the capital city Bangkok, the central plains and the Gulf of Thailand, is the country's most visited region. As such, it has long acted as a magnet for other cultures and cuisines. The influence of China is felt particularly strongly, as shown by the great number of noodle dishes eaten here. With fresh produce in abundance – be it fish and seafood from local waters, or fruit, vegetables and high-quality rice grown on the central plain – the region has something for all tastes and budgets. Its cuisine runs the gamut from elaborate platters of carved fruit and vegetables, as once served at the Royal Grand Palace, to simple but delicious street food sold from stalls to busy Bangkok office workers.

LEFT: Fresh fruit and vegetables are bartered at a floating Bangkok market – traditionally the only way to trade in Thailand.

Fragrant rice

In the central and southern regions of Thailand, steamed, fragrant rice is preferred to the sticky rice more commonly eaten in the northern and northeastern parts of the country. If you want to cook a different quantity of rice, just remember that there should always be double the volume of water to that of rice.

Ingredients
225 g (8 oz) long grain rice
600 ml (1 pint) cold water
Thai basil to garnish

Serves 4

Rinse the rice in a sieve until the water runs clear, then place it in a saucepan with the water. Bring to the boil, lower the heat and cook, uncovered, until the water has been absorbed and a series of holes appears in the surface of the rice.

Line the base of a steamer to within 1 cm (½ inch) of the edges with aluminium foil and raise the edges into a shallow, bowl-like shape. Puncture all over the base with a skewer. Turn the rice into the foil in the steamer and place over a pan of fairly fast bubbling water. Cover and cook for 30 minutes until the rice is just tender and fluffy. Refill the base pan with more boiling water as necessary.

Note that no salt is added to this recipe – this is the traditional method of cooking, as Thai rice is of such excellent quality, with a fragrant flavour, that salt is unnecessary.

Hot and sour noodle soup with shrimp

Ingredients

1 tbsp vegetable oil

2 cloves garlic, shredded

2 shallots, shredded

1 cm (½ in) fresh root ginger, thinly sliced

4–5 small red chillies, chopped

1 litre (2 pints) light chicken stock

3 kaffir lime leaves, sliced

10-cm (4-in) piece of lemongrass, chopped

200 g (7 oz) rice vermicelli

20 large shrimp, cooked, shell and head on

6 tbsp fish sauce

6 tbsp fresh lemon or lime juice

2 tbsp raw sugar

16 canned straw mushrooms

Fresh coriander and kaffir lime leaves, to
    garnish

Serves 4

*T*he hot and sour soup known as tom yum is one of Thailand's most popular and versatile dishes. This version, made with shrimp, is known as tom yum goong, but there are plenty of others, including tom yum gai (with chicken), tom yum pla (with fish) and tum yum hed (with mushrooms). The stock on which they are all based is a myriad of textures and flavours, combining sour lime leaves, sharp lemongrass, spicy ginger and fiery chillies.

Heat the oil in a frying pan. When hot, stir-fry the garlic, shallots, ginger and chillies for 1 minute. Pour in the stock, then add the lime leaves and lemongrass. Bring to a boil and simmer for 5 minutes.

Meanwhile, soak the noodles for 3 minutes in warm water, then drain and rinse under cold water. Drain before dividing the noodles among four bowls.

Add the shrimp, fish sauce, lemon juice, sugar and mushrooms to the stock and simmer for 2–3 minutes. Pour immediately over the noodles and sprinkle with coriander leaves and lime leaves.

Pork and noodle soup

*T*his Thai soup, known as kwitiaow nam, is served from floating kitchens working up and down rivers and canals. This version contains three varieties of pork, but lean cuts of pork contain only the same amount of fat as chicken. Preserved cabbage and fish balls can be bought at specialist Asian food stores.

Boil the pork loin in water for about 15 minutes. Allow it to cool before cutting into 1-cm (½-in) wide strips. Cover and set aside.

In a saucepan, boil enough water to cover the noodles and bean sprouts. Add the noodles and bean sprouts and boil for 3 minutes. Drain and divide among 4 deep bowls. Top with the pork loin, pork liver and preserved cabbage, if using.

Bring the stock to a boil. Add the fish balls and boil for 3 minutes. Remove with a slotted spoon and add to the bowls. Reserve the stock.

Put the minced pork in a saucepan with 350 ml (12 fl. oz) of chicken stock. Heat gently and stir until the pork is cooked, which should take around 4–5 minutes. Stir in the spring onions, coriander, garlic and pepper to heat through. Ladle the pork mixture and stock into the bowls. Top with the remaining heated chicken stock to fill each bowl. Serve immediately.

Ingredients

200 g (7 oz) lean pork loin, thinly sliced
300 g (11 oz) dried rice-stick noodles
325 g (12 oz) bean sprouts
100 g (4 oz) pork liver, boiled and thinly sliced
1 tsp chopped preserved cabbage (optional)
4 pints chicken stock
12 fish balls
100 g (4 oz) minced lean pork
1 spring onion, chopped
2 tbsp coarsely chopped fresh coriander
   leaves and stems
2 tbsp chopped garlic, fried in oil until
   golden
½ tsp ground white pepper

Serves 4

Stuffed baby squid in a broth

*S*quid *is a popular delicacy in Thailand where it is served as an appetizer (usually barbecued dried squid), grilled as a main course or, as in this instance, in a hot and sour broth.*

Prepare the squid by removing the heads, rubbing the purplish skin, and pulling out the quill. Turn inside out and wash well. Turn back to the original side and drain well. Cut the tentacles from the head and squeeze out the central bone. Wash and reserve tentacles.

Mix the pork, finely chopped coriander, garlic and seasoning together. Stuff the squid with this mixture, but do not overfill. Replace the tentacles at the opening of the squid. Secure with toothpicks.

Bring the fish stock to a boil with the lemongrass. Cook for a few minutes. Drop in the squid with the lime leaves and cook gently for 10–15 minutes. Remove the lemongrass and lime leaves, taste for seasoning, and add fish sauce or lime juice.

Serve in bowls topped with chilli rings and the reserved coriander leaves.

Ingredients

450 g (1 lb) baby squid, cleaned but left whole
  for stuffing
225 g (8 oz) raw pork meat, finely ground
4 stems coriander, leaves reserved for garnish
1–2 cloves garlic, peeled and crushed
Salt and freshly ground black pepper
1.5 litres (2½ pints) fish stock
2 stems of lemongrass, bruised
2 or 3 lime leaves
2 tbsp fish sauce or lime juice
1–2 chillies, seeded and cut into rings

Serves 6–8

Scallops with lemongrass broth and spinach

Scallops have very delicate flesh that quickly overcooks and becomes tough. Make sure the pan is really hot, and sear the scallops quickly on each side so they are lightly golden on the outside but soft and succulent on the inside.

Put the stock, lemongrass, spring onions, red chilli, green pepper, enoki mushrooms, sugar, fish sauce and lime juice in a saucepan and simmer for 5 minutes.

Meanwhile, heat the peanut oil in a heavy frying pan and, when very hot, sear the scallops for about 1 minute on each side until just cooked.

Add the spinach to the stock and continue to simmer until the leaves have just wilted. Divide between the serving dishes with the scallops spooned on top.

Ingredients

300 ml (10 fl. oz) chicken stock
1 tbsp lemongrass, finely sliced
4 spring onions, chopped
Red chilli, seeded and very finely chopped
½ green pepper, seeded and finely chopped
100 g (4 oz) enoki mushrooms
½ tsp caster sugar
1 tbsp fish sauce
Juice of 1 lime
2 tbsp peanut oil
12 scallops without roes
75 g (3 oz) baby spinach leaves, washed

Serves 4

Crab cakes with chilli vinegar

Ingredients
325 g (12 oz) crab meat
2 tsp red curry paste (see page 156)
1 tsp grated fresh root ginger
2 tbsp chopped fresh coriander leaves
½ tsp fish sauce
1 egg
2 tbsp plain flour
Sunflower oil, for frying

For the chilli vinegar:
1 tbsp sugar
100 ml (4 fl. oz) rice wine vinegar
2 tsp fish sauce
2 fresh red chillies, seeded and sliced

Makes 16

These spicy little fishcakes are the perfect start to a Thai meal, but they also make a great snack to serve with cocktails.

First prepare the chilli vinegar. Put the sugar, vinegar and fish sauce in a pan and warm gently, stirring, until the sugar has dissolved. Pour into a small bowl, add the chillies and set aside to cool.

Put the crab meat, curry paste, ginger, coriander and fish sauce in a bowl and mix together well using a fork. Stir in the egg, then sprinkle over the flour and mix well to combine. Shape the mixture into 16 small fishcakes.

Heat about 1 tablespoon of oil in a non-stick frying pan. Fry the fishcakes, in batches if necessary, for 2–3 minutes on each side, until golden. Drain well on paper towel and serve hot, with chilli vinegar for dipping.

There are a number of variations you can try with this dish, such as adding green curry paste (see page 150) instead of red curry paste or adding chopped lemongrass or grated lime rind to the crab cake mixture. You might also like to serve with sweet chilli sauce (see page 181) in place of chilli vinegar.

Fried mussel pancakes

*M*ussel and pancakes may seem an unlikely combination, but it works well using a batter made from tapioca flour. This is market food – if you stroll through the night market of any central Thailand town you can hear, and smell, the sizzling of this dish.

Mix all the batter ingredients together thoroughly (alternatively, you can use ready-made tempura batter). Heat a large, heavy frying pan, preferably cast iron, and add about 1 cm (½ inch) of oil.

Mix 50 g (2 oz) of the mussel meat and 50 ml (2 fl. oz) of the batter together and pour into the pan. Cook over a medium heat for about 5 minutes until brown on the bottom, then break one egg on top of the mussel cake. Flip over carefully and fry until the egg is lightly browned, which should take around 3–5 minutes. Remove the mussel cake from the pan and drain well on a paper towel. Repeat with the rest of the mussels and batter to make eight cakes.

Add the bean sprouts to the pan and fry lightly. Place on a serving plate, and arrange the mussel cakes on top. Sprinkle with the spring onions and white pepper before serving.

Serve accompanied by thick chilli sauce.

Ingredients
225 g (8 fl. oz) peanut or corn oil for frying
450 g (1 lb) raw mussel or oyster meat
8 eggs
300 g (11 oz) large bean sprouts
3 tbsp scallions, finely sliced
2 tsp ground white pepper
Thick chilli sauce, to serve

For the batter:
600 ml (1 pint) water
100 g (4 oz) plain flour
225 g (8 oz) tapioca flour or cornflour
2 tbsp baking powder
2 tbsp sugar
2 eggs, beaten
2 tsp salt

Makes 8

Stuffed crab shells

*T*his dish is as well known in Thailand for its name, poo jag, as for anything else – it means, literally, 'dear crab', for reasons that no one has ever been able to explain convincingly.

Mix all the stuffing ingredients together and fill the crab shells. Heat the oil in a frying pan or wok to approximately 180°C (350°F), or until a cube of bread dropped in turns golden in 60 seconds.

Dip the stuffed crabs in the beaten egg to coat them well all over, and then deep-fry until thoroughly cooked, for about 10–15 minutes. Remove and drain well on paper towel.

Sprinkle with the coriander and chilli before serving. Serve as an hors d'oeuvre or with steamed rice (see page 128) and bottled Asian plum sauce.

Ingredients

4 blue crab shells, well cleaned

3 eggs, beaten

1 litre (2 pints) peanut or corn oil for deep-frying

50 g (2 oz) coriander leaves

2 fresh red chillies, cut into strips lengthways

For the stuffing:

225 g (8 oz) cooked minced pork

100 g (4 oz) ground shrimp

75 g (3 oz) fresh crabmeat, or canned crabmeat, well drained

2 tbsp onion, finely chopped

1 tbsp spring onion, finely sliced

1 tsp ground white pepper

1 tsp sugar

¼ tsp light soy sauce

¼ tsp salt

Serves 4

Crab and mangetout salad

*U*se fresh white crabmeat to make the salad but pick it over carefully first in case any small sharp pieces of shell are hidden in the larger flakes of flesh.

Heat the peanut oil in a wok and stir-fry the mangetout peas, baby corn and red pepper over a medium heat for 3 minutes.

Add the beansprouts and stir-fry for a further minute, then set aside to cool.

Break up the crabmeat into large flakes. Divide the Chinese leaves between serving plates, and top with the stir-fried vegetables and then the crab.

To make the dressing, whisk all the ingredients together until the sugar has dissolved. Pour the dressing over the salad and serve.

Ingredients

2 tbsp peanut oil

175 g (6 oz) mangetout peas, thinly sliced lengthways

175 g (6 oz) baby corn, halved lengthways

½ red pepper, seeded and thinly sliced

100 g (4 oz) beansprouts

450 g (1 lb) white crabmeat

½ head of Chinese leaves (also known as napa cabbage), shredded

For the dressing:

1 red chilli, seeded and very finely chopped

½ tsp fresh ginger purée

8 tbsp sunflower oil

4 tbsp rice vinegar

2 tbsp light soy sauce

1 tsp caster sugar

Serves 4

Chicken and pomelo salad with fresh coriander, lime and green chilli dressing

Ingredients

For the dressing:

1 clove garlic, peeled and sliced

2 fresh coriander roots (if available, if not use the leaves), washed and dried

½ green chilli, seeded

150 ml (5 fl. oz) fresh lime juice

2 tsp soft light brown sugar

2 tsp fish sauce

For the salad:

1 pomelo (or use 2 grapefruit)

175 g (6 oz) cooked, peeled shrimp

325 g (12 oz) cooked chicken, shredded

3 tbsp grated fresh coconut

Fresh coriander leaves, to garnish

Serves 4

*K*nown as yam som-o, this simple chicken salad contains pomelo, a large yellow-green citrus fruit similar to a grapefruit but with a crunchier, flakier flesh. It is served with an all-purpose salad dressing called nam jim. The proportion of ingredients in this dressing will vary according to the locality and the cook's own taste, but it is important to make sure that the dressing is neither too salty nor too sweet and that the garlic is not too dominant – adjust the balance of the ingredients as required. Instead of chicken, you could use cubes of cooked white fish or baby squid mixed with the shrimp.

To make the dressing, coarsely blend the garlic and fresh coriander in a spice mill or pound in a mortar and pestle. Add the chillies and blend or pound again, then work in the lime juice. Add the sugar and fish sauce, and stir until the sugar dissolves.

Peel the pomelo, divide into segments and remove the papery skin. Break up the flesh into chunks. Place in a bowl, add the dressing and stir to mix. Add the shrimp, chicken and grated cocount and toss together lightly.

Spoon into a serving dish and garnish with fresh coriander leaves.

Rice, mango and shrimp salad with lemongrass dressing

*T*his recipe is a useful way to use up leftover cooked rice. Ensure the rice you use is less than one day old. The ingredients for the salad, which is known as khao yam paak tai, are arranged on serving plates around a mound of rice in the centre so that diners can take a little of each ingredient and mix it with the rice as they wish. Dried shrimp are available from Thai food stores.

To make the dressing, place the water in a saucepan and add the fish sauce, shrimp paste, sugar, lemongrass purée, lime zest and juice and bring to a boil. Simmer for 2 minutes, then remove from the heat and add the basil.

Place the dried shrimp in a bowl, cover with boiling water, and allow to soak for 10 minutes, then drain. Make a thin omelette with the eggs by beating the eggs together and heating them slowly on a pan. When it has a thick consistency, remove from the pan, roll up and slice thinly.

Divide the rice between four cups or small bowls, press down to shape the rice and turn the mounds out into the centre of four large serving plates.

Arrange the soaked dried shrimp, sliced omelette, mango, bean sprouts, beans, coconut, shrimp and pineapple in separate mounds around the rice and spoon the dressing over them. Garnish with the lime wedges, fresh coriander sprigs and chopped red chillies.

To serve, give each diner a small plate so they can take a little rice and mix it with a selection of individual ingredients. Serve the dressing separately if preferred.

Ingredients

For the dressing:
175 ml (5 fl oz) water
1 tbsp fish sauce
½ tsp shrimp paste (kapi)
1 tbsp soft brown sugar
1 tsp fresh lemongrass purée
Finely grated zest and juice of 1 lime
1 tbsp finely torn Thai basil

For the salad:
3 tbsp dried shrimp
2 large eggs
450 g (1 lb) cooked rice, chilled
1 under-ripe (green) mango, peeled and the flesh sliced away from the pit
100 g (4 oz) bean sprouts
100 g (4 oz) cooked green beans, sliced
4 tbsp shaved fresh coconut flesh, lightly toasted
100 g (4 oz) cooked, peeled shrimps
1 slice pineapple, cut into small pieces
Lime wedges, fresh coriander sprigs and chopped red chillies, to garnish

Serves 4

Tofu salad in garlic, chilli and lime dressing

Ingredients

100 g (4 oz) baby corn, cut into halves

275 g (10 oz) firm tofu, cut into 1 cm (½-in) cubes

50 g (2 oz) shredded iceberg lettuce

1 carrot, peeled and shredded

½ green pepper, thinly sliced

6 cherry tomatoes, halved

1 shallot, thinly sliced

3 tbsp coriander leaves

2 tbsp roasted peanuts, roughly chopped, to garnish

For the dressing:

1 clove garlic, finely chopped

½ fresh small red chilli

1 stalk lemongrass, finely chopped

1 tbsp freshly squeezed lime juice

2 tsp soft brown sugar

1 tbsp fish sauce

2 tbsp sunflower oil

Serves 4

The tofu and spicy dressing greatly enhance the taste and texture of this otherwise rather basic salad dish.

Boil the baby corn in a saucepan of boiling water for 4–5 minutes, then drain. Blanch the tofu in another pan of boiling water and drain this.

In a bowl, combine the lettuce, carrot, pepper, tomatoes, shallot, coriander, baby corn and tofu.

Place the garlic, chilli, lemongrass, lime juice, sugar, fish sauce and oil in a bowl and mix well. Pour the dressing over the salad and sprinkle with the peanuts just before serving.

LEFT: A street vendor in Bangkok mixes together a garlic, chilli and lime dressing for a fresh mango salad.

Spicy mussel salad

*Q*uick to prepare and delighfully fresh-tasting, this spicy mussel salad, known as yam hoi mang pu, is usually served in Thailand as an appetizer rather than as part of a main meal.

Steam the mussels in their shells in batches, placing a single layer of mussels in the bottom of the pan each time. Do not pile the mussels up. Steam for around 5 minutes or until all (or most) of the shells have opened. Drain and remove the meat from the opened shells. Discard any unopened shells.

In a bowl, mix together the remaining salad ingredients, except for the cabbage. Taste for seasoning, adding extra lime juice or fish sauce if required. Add the mussels and serve on a platter, with the cabbage leaves around the edge to be eaten with the salad.

Ingredients

425 g (15 oz) cooked mussel meat (from approx 1.5 kg (3 lb) mussels in their shells)
10 fresh small green chillies, finely chopped
25 g (1 oz) mint leaves
3 tbsp lime or lemon juice, or to taste
2½ tbsp fish sauce, or to taste
2 tbsp shallots, sliced
2 tbsp ginger, cut into matchsticks
2 tbsp lemongrass, finely sliced
½ tbsp kaffir lime leaves, shredded
1 small head of white Chinese (also known as napa) cabbage, cut into wedges
½ small head of green cabbage, cut into wedges

Serves 4

Scallops with Thai basil, coriander and garlic

*T*hai basil has deep-green, oval-shaped leaves with purple stems running through them. It has a much stronger flavour than the Mediterranean variety, with a strong perfume of aniseed. If you struggle to find Thai basil, substitute garlic chives. Mediterranean sweet basil could be used, but it will give the dish a different flavour.

Mix together the fish sauce, dark soy sauce and sugar until the sugar dissolves.

Heat half the peanut oil in a frying pan and fry the shallots and yellow pepper over a medium heat for 3 minutes. Add the garlic and red chilli and fry for a further 2–3 minutes until the vegetables are just tender. Remove from the pan and set aside.

Increase the heat under the pan, add the remaining oil and, when very hot, sear the scallops on each side until lightly browned.

Pour the fish sauce mixture over the scallops and stir until they are coated. Return the vegetables to the pan, add the basil and coriander, and cook for 1 minute.

Serve hot with steamed rice and a salad.

Ingredients
2 tbsp fish sauce
2 tbsp dark soy sauce
½ tsp sugar
2 tbsp peanut oil
4 red shallots, peeled and sliced
½ yellow pepper, seeded and finely chopped
2 garlic cloves, peeled and chopped
1 red chilli, seeded and chopped fine
16–20 small (queen) scallops
2 tbsp coarsely chopped Thai basil
2 tbsp coarsely chopped coriander leaves

Serves 2

Green curry paste

*T*hai cuisine has a reputation for being fiery and the country's curry dishes are no exception. Chillies are the culprit so the 'heat' of the finished dish will depend on the type of chillies used and whether you add their seeds or discard them. As a rule of thumb, the smaller the chilli, the hotter it is. Curries in Thailand are colour-coded into green, red and yellow varieties – the difference being the colour of the chillies used to make the basic curry paste. Green curries are made from fresh green chillies ground with fresh coriander, red curries from red chillies and yellow from fresh yellow chillies (or sometimes red) given a boost with ground turmeric. When the word 'gaeng' is included in the curry's title it means the sauce is based on a creamy coconut broth.

Ingredients

6 medium green chillies, seeded and coarsely chopped

2 stalks lemongrass, outer leaves removed and chopped

Small bunch fresh coriander, stalks removed

Small bunch Thai basil, stalks removed

1 shallot, peeled and chopped

1 tsp coriander seeds

1 tsp cumin seeds

2 large cloves garlic, peeled and coarsely chopped

1 tsp shrimp paste (kapi)

2.5-cm (1-in) piece fresh galangal, peeled and chopped or 2 tsp galangal purée

4 kaffir lime leaves, chopped

Makes 120 ml (4 fl. oz)

Put all the ingredients in a food processor and blend to a paste. Alternatively, pound the ingredients using a pestle and mortar.

Store the paste in a sealed container in the refrigerator and use as needed. It will keep for up to 3 weeks.

Green beef curry

*D*efinitely green, this is one of the basic Thai curry styles, and can be used equally well to make a curry with pork, chicken or duck instead of beef.

Heat 300 ml (½ pint) of the coconut milk in a pan, add the chilli paste and cook for 2 minutes. Add the beef and the rest of the coconut milk, and bring to a boil.

Add the fish sauce and palm sugar, boil for 2 more minutes, then add the aubergine and chilli and cook for 1 minute. Stir in the lime leaf, boil for 1 minute, add the basil and remove from the heat.

Serve in bowls accompanied by steamed rice, pickled vegetables, salted eggs and sun-dried beef.

Ingredients

1 litre (2 pints) thin coconut milk

Green chilli paste (see opposite)

300 g (11 oz) beef sirloin, cut into
    2.5 x 2 x 0.5 cm (1 x ¾ x ¼ in) slices

2 tbsp fish sauce

½ tbsp palm sugar (or dark muscovado sugar)

10 small white aubergines, quartered

3 fresh red chillies, quartered lengthways

3 kaffir lime leaves, torn into small pieces

2 tbsp sweet basil leaves

Serves 4

Green curry with shrimp, pumpkin and courgette

*N*ot all green curries are the same – there's plenty of room for variation around the basic theme. This shrimp-based recipe uses pumpkin and courgette to give added texture. The Thai basil garnish provides a pleasant, aniseed-like aroma.

Heat the peanut oil in a large frying pan, add the shallot and pumpkin or butternut squash, and fry for 5 minutes, stirring occasionally.

Add the courgette and green curry paste and fry for a further 2 minutes, stirring to make sure the paste does not stick.

Stir in the fish sauce, sugar and coconut milk. Bring to a boil, lower the heat and simmer for 15 minutes until the pumpkin or butternut squash is tender.

Add the shrimp and simmer for 2–3 minutes until they turn pink. Serve garnished with the spring onions, green chilli and Thai basil leaves.

Ingredients

2 tbsp peanut oil

3 red shallots, peeled and sliced

200 g (7 oz) pumpkin or butternut squash, peeled, seeded and cut into small pieces

1 courgette, sliced

2 tbsp green chilli paste (see page 150)

1 tbsp fish sauce

1 tbsp soft brown sugar

400 ml (14 fl. oz) coconut milk

450 g (1 lb) raw peeled shrimp

2 spring onions, shredded

1 green chilli, seeded and finely sliced

Thai basil leaves

Serves 4

Green curry with chicken

Ingredients

2 tbsp peanut oil

2 shallots, peeled and sliced

1 sweet potato, peeled and cut into small
  pieces

1 courgette, trimmed and sliced

2 tbsp green curry paste (see page 150)

500 g (1 lb 2 oz) boneless chicken thighs,
  skinned and cut into chunks

1 tbsp fish sauce

2 tbsp palm sugar (or dark muscovado sugar)

400 ml (14 fl. oz) coconut milk

3 kaffir lime leaves, shredded, to garnish

1 red chilli, seeded and finely sliced, to
  garnish

Serves 6

This is the most famous and most widely eaten of all the green curry recipes, known in Thailand as gaeng kheow wan gai. Despite its fame, it still allows for a good deal of flexibility. A selection of firm white fish or shellfish can easily be substituted for the chicken without needing to change the basic recipe – simply make sure that you add the fish or shellfish around 5 minutes before the curry is cooked, so that it will not overcook and become tough and tasteless. Also, avoid stirring the curry too frequently once the white fish has been added or its delicate flesh will break and disintegrate.

Heat the oil in a large saucepan, add the shallots and sweet potato, and fry over a gentle heat for 5 minutes, stirring occasionally. Add the courgette and curry paste and fry for a further 2 minutes.

Add the chicken, stirring so it is evenly coated in the spice paste, and fry for 5 minutes.

Stir in the fish sauce, sugar and coconut milk and bring to a boil.

Lower the heat and simmer gently for 15 minutes until the chicken and sweet potato are done and the sauce has reduced and thickened a little.

Serve at once garnished with the shredded lime leaves and chilli.

Fried vermicelli with red curry paste

Though it may look more fiery, there is no reason why red curry paste should be any hotter than the green version. Its precise heat level is entirely down to your own personal taste – remember more chillies equals more heat. If you really feel like testing your tastebuds, try adding the chilli seeds as well.

To make the curry paste, put all the ingredients in a food processor and blend to a paste. Alternatively, pound the ingredients using a pestle and mortar.

Soak the rice vermicelli in warm water for 3–5 minutes. Rinse, and drain.

Heat the oil in a wok or frying pan, and fry the tofu until golden brown. Add the garlic, bamboo shoots, bean sprouts and mustard greens or spinach, stirring each time you add the ingredients.

Add the red curry paste, fish sauce, soy sauce and sugar and stir well. Add the vermicelli and stir until the noodles are well coated with the sauce. Divide the vermicelli between four plates and garnish with the coriander leaves and lime wedges. Serve at once.

Ingredients

For the paste:

4–6 medium red chillies, seeded (optional) and coarsely chopped

50 g (2 oz) shallots, coarsely chopped

1 tbsp coriander root (or fresh leaves)

2 kaffir lime leaves

2 stalks lemongrass, outer leaves removed, coarsely chopped

1 tsp coriander seeds

1 tsp cumin seeds

2 large cloves garlic, coarsely chopped

1 tbsp shrimp paste (kapi)

1 tbsp galangal purée or 2.5-cm (1-in) piece of fresh root ginger, coarsely chopped

2 cloves garlic, peeled and chopped

¼ tsp salt

For the noodles:

225 g (8 oz) rice vermicelli

3 tbsp vegetable oil

225 g (8 oz) tofu (bean curd), diced

3 cloves garlic, chopped

100 g (4 oz) canned bamboo shoots

700 g (1½ lb) bean sprouts

225 g (8 oz) mustard greens or fresh spinach

2 tbsp red curry paste

6 tbsp fish sauce

3 tbsp light soy sauce

1 tbsp palm sugar (or dark muscovado sugar)

Coriander leaves, to garnish

4 lime wedges, to garnish

Serves 4

Red curry with tofu

Ingredients

Salt

½ aubergine, chopped

1 tbsp sunflower oil

1 clove garlic, finely chopped

1 shallot, sliced

325 g (12 oz) firm tofu, diced into 2.5-cm (1-in) cubes

100 g (4 oz) canned bamboo shoots

2 tbsp red curry paste (see page 156)

400 ml (14 fl. oz) coconut milk

2 tbsp fish sauce

1 tsp soft brown sugar

1 kaffir lime leaf

1 tsp freshly squeezed lime juice

1 tbsp coriander leaves, for garnish

Steamed rice, to serve (see page 28)

Serves 4

*T*his recipe has been influenced by both Thai and Chinese cooking. The result is a novel combination of heat and sourness.

Sprinkle the salt over the aubergine pieces and leave for 15–20 minutes before lightly rinsing. Heat the oil in a frying pan and fry the garlic and shallot for 1 minute.

Add the tofu, bamboo shoots and red curry paste, and stir-fry for 1 minute.

Add the coconut milk, fish sauce, sugar, lime leaf and lime juice. Bring to the boil, then simmer for 15–20 minutes.

Garnish with coriander and serve with steamed rice.

Red vegetable curry with squash and sweet potato

*T*his curry can be served on its own as a vegetarian meal or as an accompaniment to a spicy meat or fish dish. Be sure to cut the squash and sweet potato into small pieces so that they cook quickly and evenly.

Heat the peanut oil in a deep frying pan or large saucepan, add the red curry paste and onion and fry over a low heat for 2–3 minutes until the onion starts to soften. Add the sweet potato and butternut squash and fry for a further 10 minutes, stirring occasionally.

Add the green pepper, courgette and shiitake mushrooms, fry for 2 minutes, then add the fish sauce, lime juice, sugar, lemongrass and coconut milk.

Cover the pan and leave the curry to simmer gently for 10–15 minutes or until the vegetables are tender. Garnish with the red onion, red chilli and coconut. Serve with steamed rice.

Ingredients

2 tbsp peanut oil

2 tbsp red curry paste (see page 156)

1 red onion, peeled and sliced

1 sweet potato, peeled and cut into 1-cm (¾-in) dice

200 g (7 oz) butternut squash, peeled, seeded and cut into 1-cm (¾-in) dice

1 green pepper, seeded and chopped

1 courgette, chopped

100 g (4 oz) shiitake mushrooms, sliced

2 tbsp fish sauce

1 tbsp lime juice

2 tsp caster sugar

1 tsp lemongrass, sliced fine

350 ml (12 fl. oz) coconut milk

1 tbsp red onion, finely chopped, to garnish

1 red chilli, seeded and finely chopped

2 tbsp shredded fresh coconut or desiccated coconut, to garnish

Steamed rice, to serve (see page 128)

Serves 4

Sweet and sour chicken

Ingredients

225 g (8 fl. oz) peanut or corn oil
425 (15 oz) skinless, boneless chicken breasts,
    cut across into 5 mm (¼-in) slices
Plain flour, for coating
1 medium-sized onion, sliced
1 medium-sized green pepper, sliced
3 tbsp ketchup
1 large carrot, thinly chopped
100 g (4 oz) tomato quarters
100 g (4 oz) pineapple, chopped
100 ml (4 fl. oz) chicken stock
2 tsp light soy sauce
1 tsp sugar
1 tsp vinegar
Steamed rice, to serve (see page 128)

Serves 4–6

A Thai take on this popular Asian dish. It is not an overly spicy recipe, but a spoonful of fish sauce will add zest.

Heat the oil in a wok or frying pan, coat the chicken lightly with flour, and fry it until it is light brown, which should take around 5 minutes. Remove and drain on paper towel.

Discard all the oil except for about 4 tablespoons. Add the onion and pepper, cook for 1 minute. Mix in the ketchup, and then add the remaining ingredients. Stir-fry for 1 minute, add the chicken, and continue to cook until the onion is tender, which should take about 2 minutes.

Serve accompanied by steamed rice and fish sauce with fresh chillies (see page 28).

Fried rice-stick noodles with shrimp

*A*lso known as pad thai, this is the best-known of all Thai noodle dishes. The key to a tasty pad thai lies in the use of salty dried shrimp and roasted peanuts. Adjust the amount of chilli used to suit your palate. It is quick and easy to prepare, and is usually eaten as a secondary rather than as a main dish.

Mix together the marinade ingredients, and marinate the shrimp for at least 15 minutes.

Soak the noodles in warm water for 2–5 minutes, or according to the instructions on the package. Rinse under cold water and drain.

Heat 2 tablespoons of the oil in a wok or frying pan, and stir-fry the garlic and shallots for 30 seconds. Make a well in the middle and pour in the eggs. Lightly scramble without incorporating the garlic and shallots. Stir in the peanuts, chillies, dried shrimp, spring onions and bean sprouts.

Add 1 tablespoon of oil to the wok, and stir in the noodles. Add the sugar, fish sauce and lemon juice, and stir to coat the noodles. Push to one side while the marinated shrimp are stir-fried in the remaining tablespoon of oil.

Divide the noodles among four plates and top with the shrimp, coriander leaves and lime wedges. Serve immediately.

Ingredients

For the marinade:

1 tsp freshly squeezed lemon juice

1 tsp fish sauce

½ tsp soft brown sugar

12 large cooked shrimps, shelled and deveined, tails intact

275 g (10 oz) dried, rice-stick noodles

4 tbsp vegetable oil

3 cloves garlic, crushed

4 shallots, sliced

2 eggs, beaten

2 tbsp roasted peanuts, crushed

3–4 small green chillies, chopped

2 tbsp dried shrimp, chopped

2 spring onions, chopped

200 g (7 oz) bean sprouts

2½ tbsp soft brown sugar

6 tbsp fish sauce

100 ml (4 fl. oz) freshly squeezed lemon juice

Fresh coriander leaves, to garnish

4 lime wedges, to garnish

Serves 2

Casseroled shrimp with bean-thread noodles

*T*his recipe, known as kung op woon sen in Thailand, makes four generous servings. The size of the shrimp is unimportant, and lobster tails or crab claws can be substituted. But for maximum flavour, use fresh, not frozen, produce.

Place the soup stock ingredients in a pan and bring to a boil. Simmer for 5 minutes, then set aside to cool.

In a heatproof casserole dish or heavy saucepan, lay out the bacon so that it covers the base. Top with the shrimp, coriander root, ginger, garlic and peppercorns. Cover with noodles, then add the butter, soy sauce and soup stock.

Place on the heat, cover, and bring to a boil. Simmer for 5 minutes, then mix well, and sprinkle with chopped coriander. Cover and cook for 5 minutes, or until the shrimp are cooked through. Remove any excess soup stock before serving.

Ingredients

For the soup stock:
600 ml (1 pint) chicken stock
2 tbsp oyster sauce
1½ tbsp dark soy sauce
½ tbsp sesame oil
½ tsp sugar

For the shrimp and noodles:
2 bacon strips, cut into 2.5-cm (1-in) pieces
20 large fresh shrimp, shelled
  and deveined
2 fresh coriander roots, rinsed and halved
25 g (1 oz) fresh root ginger, finely chopped
1 clove garlic, chopped
1 tsp white peppercorns, crushed
225 g (8 oz) bean-thread noodles (also known
  as cellophane or glass noodles), soaked
  in hot water for 5 minutes
1 tsp butter
2 tbsp dark soy sauce
2 tbsp fresh coriander, roughly chopped

Serves 4

Sweet crisp-fried vermicelli with shrimp and cashew nuts

Although it requires a little more time than most noodle dishes, this rice vermicelli dish is well worth the extra effort. It is essential that it is served as soon as it is ready as the vermicelli will become mushy if left for very long.

Heat the vegetable oil in a wok or saucepan until very hot. Deep-fry the vermicelli for a few seconds until they puff up and become white. Drain on paper towel.

Heat the tablespoon of oil in a wok or frying pan. Add the garlic and shallots, and stir. Add the shrimp and cashew nuts, and stir-fry for about 2 minutes.

Add the sugar, lemon juice, vinegar, soy sauce, ketchup and chilli powder and simmer until the sauce thickens. Take out the shrimp, and set aside.

Add the crisp vermicelli, and coat with the sauce. Arrange the vermicelli on a bed of lettuce on four plates. Top each serving with three shrimp, and garnish with coriander and tomato wedges.

Ingredients

For the sauce:

3 tbsp palm sugar (or dark muscovado sugar)

2 tbsp freshly squeezed lemon juice

1 tsp vinegar

1 tsp light soy sauce

2 tbsp tomato ketchup

½ tsp chilli powder

For the noodles:

Vegetable oil for deep-frying

50 g (2 oz) rice vermicelli, slightly crushed

1 tbsp vegetable oil

2 cloves garlic, finely chopped

2 shallots, finely chopped

12 tiger or jumbo shrimp with tails, peeled and deveined

4 tbsp raw cashew nuts

2 lettuce leaves, halved

Coriander leaves, to garnish

2 small tomato wedges, to garnish

Serves 4

Sweet crisp-fried vermicelli with shrimp, pork and tofu

*T*his is a Thai embellishment of a Chinese dish, and for complete success depends on the noodles being fried just right – so that they are both crisp and puffy when served.

Heat the oil in a frying pan or wok and fry the shrimp and pork until brown and well cooked, which should take about 10 minutes.

Remove with a slotted spoon and drain on paper towel. Set aside.

Add the tofu to the hot oil and fry until brown, which should take around 2 minutes. Remove with a slotted spoon and drain on paper towel.

Add the noodles to the hot oil and brown lightly for around 4–5 minutes. Remove and drain well on paper towel.

Discard all the oil from the pan except for 2 tablespoons. Add the garlic and onion and fry gently for 1 minute; then add pork, shrimp, tofu, palm sugar, vinegar, marinated soybeans and fish sauce. Fry until thick and sticky, which should take around 7–10 minutes.

Reduce the heat and add the noodles. Mix well for 1 minute, then transfer on to a large plate and arrange in a mound. Place the bean sprouts, spring onions, pickled garlic and chillies on top.

Ingredients

Peanut or corn oil for deep-frying
200 g (7 oz) raw medium-sized shrimps, shelled and cut into 3 pieces
150 g (5 oz) pork loin, cut into cubes the same size as the shrimp pieces
100 g (4 oz) firm tofu (bean curd), cut into small rectangles
150 g (5 oz) thin rice vermicelli noodles, if dried soak first in cool water for 1 minute
½ tbsp garlic, chopped
½ tbsp onion, chopped
50 g (2 oz) palm sugar (or dark muscovado sugar)
2 tbsp white vinegar
1 tbsp marinated soybeans
1 tbsp fish sauce
700 g (1½ lb) bean sprouts
3 spring onions, cut into 4-cm (1½-in) pieces
2 tbsp pickled garlic, sliced
2 fresh red chillies, cut into very thin strips.

Serves 4–6

Grilled swordfish with lime and coriander

Ingredients

4 x 175-g (6-oz) swordfish steaks

1 tbsp peanut oil

1 tbsp fish sauce

2 tbsp dark soy sauce

2 tsp soft brown sugar

2 tbsp freshly squeezed lime juice

2 tbsp chopped fresh coriander

1 red chilli, seeded and very finely sliced

75 g (3 oz) fresh spinach leaves

Lemon or lime wedges, to garnish

Serves 2

Fish and citrus fruits make natural partners, and fresh lime goes particularly well with an oily, firm-fleshed fish like swordfish. Serve accompanied with spinach.

Place the swordfish steaks side by side in a shallow dish. Mix the peanut oil, fish sauce, dark soy sauce, brown sugar, lime juice, coriander leaves and red chilli together, and pour over the fish. Cover and leave to marinate in a cool place for 1–2 hours.

Lift the fish from the marinade, place on a grill rack or in a hot ridged grill pan and cook for 2–3 minutes on each side, depending on the thickness of the steaks, until just cooked through.

Meanwhile, pour the marinade left in the dish into a wok and boil until reduced by half. Add the spinach leaves and simmer until wilted.

Spoon the spinach onto serving plates, place the swordfish steaks on top and spoon over any juices left in the wok. Serve garnished with lemon or lime pieces.

'Jackfruit seeds'

These sweet candies are one of a range of Thai sweetmeats made with mung beans and egg yolks. Kanoon, or jackfruit, is not used in the recipe – they are only called after the fruit because of their similar shapes.

Ingredients

450 g (1 lb) dried yellow mung beans

1 kg (2½ lb) sugar

1.25 litres (2 pints) thin coconut milk

1.5 litres (2½ pints) water

10 egg yolks, duck if possible, whisked lightly

Serves 6–8

Soak the mung beans in water for 1 hour, then drain and steam them for 20 minutes or until soft. Mash or purée in a food processor.

Put the beans in a pan with half of the sugar and the coconut milk. Bring to a boil and then simmer, stirring, until reduced to a paste. This should take about 15 minutes – be careful not to burn the mixture. Remove from the heat and leave to cool.

Meanwhile, make the syrup. Boil the water with the remaining sugar until reduced by half. Remove 225 ml (8 fl. oz) of the syrup and reserve. Keep the remaining syrup simmering slowly.

Take pieces of the bean paste and shape them into small fingertip-sized ovals. Cook them in batches of 8–10 at a time. Dip them first into the egg yolk and then drop them into the pan of syrup. Wait until they float to the top, then remove with a slotted spoon and drain on paper towel. Place them in the reserved syrup for 30 minutes, remove, set aside and allow to dry for 5 minutes.

Serve immediately or cover and refrigerate; serve at room temperature.

CHAPTER FIVE

Southern Thailand

Three influences dominate the cuisine of southern Thailand: climate, coastline and neighbouring countries. Coconuts grow well in the south's tropical heat and their various elements – the milk, the flesh and the oil – feature in many dishes. Every day, the region's fishing boats haul ashore a great wealth of fish and seafood, more of which is eaten here than in any other part of the country. However, the large Muslim population means that little pork is consumed. The culinary heritage of surrounding countries, particularly India, is shown in the south's fondness for fiercely spiced curries, while the popularity of satay and other dishes that feature peanuts, can be traced back to Indonesia, to the region's south.

Chumpon Province
Ranong Province
Prachuap Khiri Khan Province
Surat Thani Province
Phangnga Province
Krabi Province
Nakhon Si Thammarat Province
Phuket Province
Phatthalung Province
Pattani Province
Songkhla Province
Yala Province
Satun Province
Trang Province
Narathiwat Province

LEFT: Fishing boats at dusk off a beach in Koh Samui – one of the largest islands off the coast of southern Thailand.

Coconut and galangal soup

*T*his creamy soup is a firm favourite on southern Thailand's restaurant menus, not least because of the delicate aroma and flavour provided by the galangal.

Pour the coconut milk into a pan and bring to a boil. Add the shallots, galangal, lemongrass, chilli, lime leaf and salt.

Bring to a boil, add the chicken and then bring to a boil again. Add the mushrooms and bring it back to a boil for a final 2 minutes.

Remove from the heat and stir in the lime juice, fish sauce and coriander.

Serve in bowls accompanied by rice, lime wedges and fish sauce with chillies (see page 28).

Ingredients

1.5 litres (2½ pints) thin coconut milk

25 g (1 oz) shallots, finely chopped

15 g (½ oz) galangal, finely sliced

2 stalks lemongrass, cut into 2-cm (¾-in) pieces

6 fresh small whole red chillies

3 kaffir lime leaves, torn into small pieces

1 tsp salt

300 g (11 oz) skinless, boneless chicken breasts, cut across into 6-mm (¼-in) thick slices

200 g (7 oz) fresh mushrooms (oyster if available)

2 tbsp lime or lemon juice

½ tbsp fish sauce

3 tbsp coriander leaves and stems cut into 2-cm (¾-in) pieces

Serves 4–6

Chicken satay

Ingredients

450 g (1 lb) skinless, boneless chicken breasts, cut into 7.5 x 2 x 0.5-cm (3 x ¾ x ¼-in) long slices

350 ml (12 fl. oz) thin coconut milk

5 kaffir lime leaves, roughly chopped

5 coriander roots, crushed

2 stalks of lemongrass, roughly chopped

1 tbsp curry powder

1 tsp palm sugar (or dark muscovado sugar)

½ tsp salt

Toasted of sliced bread, to serve

For the satay sauce:

75 g (3 oz) dried yellow mung beans

1.5 litres (2½ pints) thin coconut milk

225 g (8 oz) unsalted roasted peanuts, very finely chopped

100 g (4 oz) red chilli paste (see page 51)

50 g (2 oz) red curry paste (see page 156)

3 tbsp palm sugar (or dark muscovado sugar)

2 tsp tamarind juice

1 tsp salt

For the ajaad salad:

600 ml (1 pint) white vinegar

75 g (3 oz) sugar

1 tsp salt

1 small cucumber, quartered and sliced lengthways

50 g (2 oz) shallots, sliced

2 fresh red chillies, thinly sliced into rings

Serves 4–6

Now popular all over Thailand, and a speciality of market food stalls, satay arrived in the south from Indonesia, via Malaysia. The dish can be made just as well with pork, tiger shrimp, tofu or beef. Serve accompanied by a Thai ajaad salad.

Mix the chicken slices with all the other ingredients in a bowl and leave to marinate for 3–4 hours. Then carefully skewer the meat onto wood or metal skewers and grill, preferably over charcoal.

While the chicken is marinating, make the satay sauce. Soak the mung beans in water for 1 hour, then drain and steam them for 20 minutes or until soft. Purée in a food processor. Mix the mung bean purée and all the remaining satay sauce ingredients together and boil in a pan or wok for 5 minutes. Remove from the heat and leave to cool.

To make the ajaad salad, simmer the vinegar, sugar and salt together in a pan until reduced to about 225 ml (8 fl. oz). Remove from the heat, cool and mix with the cucumber, shallots and chillies.

Serve the chicken skewers with the satay sauce, ajaad salad and slices of toasted bread.

Sweetcorn cakes with peanut sauce

If serving the peanut sauce cold, remember it will thicken upon standing so you will need to stir in a few tablespoons of warm water to thin it down to the right consistency.

In a bowl, mix together the corn, green curry paste, fish sauce, brown sugar, coriander and mangetout peas. Stir in the flour until the ingredients are coated and then the egg to bind them together.

To make the sauce, heat the oil in a saucepan and fry the onion until softened. Add the garlic and chilli and cook for 1 minute, then stir in the peanut butter, brown sugar, fish sauce and coconut milk. Heat gently, stirring frequently so the ingredients are evenly combined.

Heat the oil for deep-frying to 180°C (350°F), or until a cube of bread dropped in turns golden in 60 seconds. Drop tablespoons of the sweetcorn mixture into the hot oil and fry for 3–4 minutes until golden brown. Drain and serve with the peanut sauce, and garnished with the chopped chilli, spring onions, coriander sprigs and extra sweetcorn kernels.

Ingredients

For the cakes:
8 mangetout peas, finely chopped
100 g (4 oz) corn kernels with peppers
1 tbsp green curry paste (see page 150)
1 tbsp fish sauce
1 tsp soft brown sugar
1 tbsp chopped fresh coriander
75 g (3 oz) plain flour
1 egg, beaten
Oil for deep-frying

For the peanut sauce:
1 small onion, finely chopped
1 garlic clove, crushed
1 small red chilli, seeded and finely chopped
1 tbsp oil
4 tbsp crunchy peanut butter
2 tsp soft brown sugar
1 tsp fish sauce
100 ml (4 fl. oz) coconut milk

For the garnish:
Red chilli, finely chopped
Spring onions, shredded
Coriander sprigs
Sweetcorn kernels

Serves 4–6

Deep-fried tempeh with sweet chilli sauce

Ingredients

For the sauce:
100 ml (4 fl. oz) rice vinegar
100 g (4 oz) sugar
3 large, pasilla chillies (see page 20), seeded
¼ cucumber, peeled, seeded and grated

For the tempeh:
325 g (12 oz) tempeh
Oil for deep-frying
2 butter lettuce leaves
1 tomato, sliced, to garnish
4 cm (1½ in) cucumber, sliced

Serves 4

*S*weet chilli sauce is the usual condiment served with snacks sold at street food stalls in Thailand. It is packaged in small plastic bags for dipping on the go, or for pouring over a more leisurely sit-down snack. Like tofu, tempeh is made from soybeans – but tempeh is a whole soybean product with a firmer texture and a stronger flavour.

To make the chilli sauce, put the vinegar and sugar in a saucepan and heat gently until the sugar dissolves. Add the chillies and simmer for 10 minutes. Remove from the heat. Once cool, purée in a blender or food processor and then stir in the grated cucumber.

Cut the tempeh in half, then slice into 2.5-cm (1-in) pieces. Heat the oil to 180°C (325°F), or until a cube of bread dropped in turns golden in 60 seconds.

Deep-fry the tempeh for about 5 minutes or until golden brown. Drain well on paper towel. Arrange the tempeh on a bed of lettuce and garnish with the sliced tomato and cucumber.

Serve the chilli sauce in a small side dish.

Tempeh and vegetable salad with peanut dressing

*T*he secret of this recipe is to stop cooking the vegetables when they are still crisp rather than waiting until they get too soft.

Heat the oil in a frying pan. Shallow-fry the tempeh until golden brown. Drain thoroughly on paper towel.

Cook the baby corn, carrots, courgette and bean sprouts in a pan of boiling water for 3–4 minutes. Add the pepper for the final minute. Drain well.

Mix the peanut butter, soy sauce, sugar, lemon juice, water and chilli powder together and shake well in a jar.

Place the lettuce and sliced tomatoes on a serving plate and arrange the blanched vegetables and tempeh on the top. Drizzle the peanut dressing over the salad.

Serve immediately.

Ingredients
Oil for shallow-frying
325 g (12 oz) tempeh, cut into bite-sized
 pieces
225 g (8 oz) baby corn, cut into halves
225 g (8 oz) carrot, peeled and shredded
1 courgette, shredded
225 g (8 oz) bean sprouts, rinsed
1 green pepper, seeded and sliced

For the peanut dressing:
6 tbsp peanut butter
2 tbsp light soy sauce
3 tbsp sugar
3 tbsp freshly squeezed lemon juice
100 ml (4 fl. oz) water
¼ tsp ground chilli powder
Butter lettuce and sliced tomatoes,
 to garnish

Serves 4

RIGHT: Fishing boats in the town of Krabi, southern Thailand. With access to the Krabi River and the Andamon Sea, this is an ideal spot for fresh seafood.

Fishcakes with sweet chilli dipping sauce

Ingredients

225 g (8 oz) salmon fillet, skinned

225 g (8 oz) firm white fish fillet, such as
  flounder, sole or monkfish, skinned

1 tsp fresh ginger purée

1 tsp fresh lemongrass purée

2 kaffir lime leaves, very finely shredded

1 tbsp fish sauce

100 g (4 oz) fine green beans, trimmed and
  finely chopped

1 tbsp chopped fresh coriander

1 egg white, lightly beaten

Oil, for shallow-frying

Lime wedges, to garnish

Sweet chilli sauce, to serve (see page 180)

Makes 20

*T*aud mun is the Thai name for these tiny, bite-sized fishcakes. They make an excellent snack to serve with drinks or as an appetizer. In this recipe, salmon and white fish are mixed with spices and lime leaves, but different combinations of fish can be used. You can use all white fish rather than a mix of white and salmon, or replace some of the fish with white crabmeat, prepared squid or raw, medium-sized shrimp if you prefer. The lime, however, is an important flavouring in this recipe, so if you cannot find fresh lime leaves, use the finely grated rind of two limes instead.

Cut the salmon and white fish into chunks and place in a food processor with the ginger purée, lemongrass purée and lime leaves. Mix until coarsely ground.

Transfer to a bowl and stir in the fish sauce, green beans, fresh coriander and egg white.

Shape into small balls and then flatten into cakes roughly 1-cm (½-in) thick. Shallow-fry in hot oil for 2 minutes each side until golden. Drain on paper towel and serve garnished with lime wedges and accompanied by the sweet chilli dipping sauce.

Spicy fishcakes with coriander soy dipping sauce

A mixture of salmon and a firm white fish, such as cod, is used here but you could just use salmon if you prefer. These are perhaps best served as a starter with a small salad garnish and the dipping sauce spooned over.

Cut the salmon and white fish into chunks. Trim and finely chop the green beans.

Place the salmon, white fish, lemongrass purée, ginger purée and lime zest in a food processor and whizz until coarsely ground – be careful not to reduce the mixture to a paste. Transfer to a bowl and stir in the fish sauce, coriander, green beans and egg white.

With floured hands, shape into small balls and flatten into round cakes, about 1 cm (½-in) thick. Chill for 1 hour.

To make the dipping sauce, toast the coriander seeds in a dry, heavy-bottomed frying pan until golden. Remove from the pan and mix with the soy sauce, vinegar and sugar, stirring until the sugar dissolves. Pour into a serving bowl and float a few fresh coriander leaves on top.

Heat oil for deep-frying to 180°C (350°F), or until a cube of bread dropped in turns golden in 60 seconds. Fry in batches for 2–3 minutes until golden. Drain and serve with the dipping sauce.

Ingredients

225 g (8 oz) salmon fillet, skinned
225 g (8 oz) firm white fish fillet, such as haddock or plaice
100 g (4 oz) fine green beans
1 tsp fresh lemongrass purée
1 tsp fresh ginger purée
Zest of 1 lime, finely grated
1 tbsp fish sauce
1 tbsp chopped fresh coriander
1 egg white, lightly beaten
Plain flour, to dust
Oil, for deep-frying

For the dipping sauce:
1 tbsp coriander seeds
4 tbsp dark soy sauce
1 tbsp white wine vinegar
½ tsp sugar
Fresh coriander leaves, chopped

Makes 20

Shrimp skewers with coconut rice

Ingredients

40 g (1½ oz) raw tiger shrimp, peeled and deveined but tails left on
1 tsp fresh lemongrass purée
1 tsp fresh galangal purée
2 tsp green chilli paste (see page 150)
1 tbsp fish sauce
25 g (1 oz) creamed coconut
900 ml (1½ pints) vegetable stock
225 g (8 oz) Thai fragrant rice (see page 128)
2 tbsp chopped fresh coriander
1 green chilli, seeded and chopped fine

Serves 4

These tangy shrimp skewers work very well served with steamed, fragrant rice and enlivened with a little bit of creamed coconut.

Thread the tiger shrimp onto skewers and place side-by-side in a shallow dish.

Mix together the lemongrass purée, galangal purée, chilli paste and fish sauce and spread over the shrimp. Cover and leave to marinate for 1 hour.

Place the creamed coconut and vegetable stock in a large saucepan and heat gently until the coconut dissolves. Rinse the Thai fragrant rice in a colander under cold running water, then add to the saucepan of simmering stock.

Simmer for 10–12 minutes or until the rice is tender and has absorbed the stock.

While the rice is cooking, heat the grill to high. Line the grill rack with foil and place the shrimp skewers on it in a single layer. Grill for 5 minutes until the shrimp turn pink, turning the skewers over halfway.

Stir the coriander and chopped green chilli into the coconut rice, and serve with the shrimp skewers.

Mussel and shrimp fritters

A popular street food in Bangkok, these fritters can be bought from road-side vendors who cook them fresh for customers. Use large mussels such as greenlip, and be sure to heat the oil to the correct temperature before you fry.

To make the fritters, sift the plain flour and the baking powder into a mixing bowl. Make a well in the centre, pour in half the beer and stir until mixed well. Gradually whisk in the rest of the beer to make a smooth batter. Set aside to stand for 1 hour.

Dust the mussels and shrimp lightly in flour, and heat the oil for deep-frying to 180°C (350°F), or until a cube of bread dropped in turns golden after 60 seconds.

To make the dipping sauce, stir the ingredients together in a small bowl until the sugar dissolves.

Add a few mussels and shrimp to the batter, lift them out with tongs or a fork and allow the excess batter to run back into the bowl. Add them to the hot oil and deep-fry for 2–3 minutes or until they are golden and crisp.

Drain the mussels and shrimp on paper towel and fry the rest in batches in the same way. Serve the fritters hot with the dipping sauce.

Ingredients

For the fritters:
225 g (8 oz) plain flour, plus extra to dust
½ tsp baking powder
225 ml (8 fl. oz) light beer
12 large mussels, such as greenlip
12 large raw shrimp, peeled
Peanut oil, for deep-frying

For the dipping sauce:
2 tbsp fish sauce
2 tbsp lime juice
½ tsp sweet chilli sauce (see page 180)
1 tsp caster sugar

Serves 4

Spicy seafood salad with sea bass

Ingredients

150 g (5 oz) sea bass, cleaned, gutted and
  thinly sliced into strips
150 g (5 oz) large shrimp, shelled
150 g (5 oz) squid, body and tentacles,
  cleaned, gutted and sliced into 2-cm (¾-in)
  strips
7 fresh small green chillies
5 garlic cloves
2 coriander roots
2 tbsp fish sauce
½ tsp sugar
2 tbsp lime or lemon juice
4 spring onions, sliced into 5-mm (¼-in) pieces
100 g (4 oz) onion, thinly sliced
50 g (2 oz) celery leaves and stalks, sliced

Serves 6

*T*he Thai version of a seafood salad is a flavourful assembly of different ingredients quite unlike those featured in western salads. Most are extremely spicy. This dish combines three of the basic flavours: spicy, sour and salty.

Cook the fish, shrimp and squid separately in salted water for about 2–3 minutes each, and then drain.

Pound the chillies, garlic, coriander root, fish sauce and sugar together with a mortar and pestle or in a food processor until finely blended.

Place this mixture in a bowl and mix in the lemon juice, spring onions, onion and celery. Stir in the fish and seafood and mix well. Serve immediately.

Lime-dressed shrimp salad

Choose green, unripe mangoes for this salad because ripe,
golden-fleshed ones will be too sweet and have too soft a texture.

For the dressing, mix the ingredients together until the sugar dissolves. Set aside.

To make the salad, heat the sunflower oil in a wok and stir-fry the tiger shrimp for 1–2 minutes until they turn pink. Transfer to a bowl and pour over the dressing, stirring so all the shrimp are coated. Leave to cool.

Arrange the salad leaves, mango, red pepper and cucumber on a serving dish and spoon the shrimp and dressing over the top.

Serve with lime wedges to squeeze over.

Ingredients

For the dressing:
5 tbsp sunflower oil
Juice of 2 limes
2 tbsp light soy sauce
½ tsp caster sugar

For the salad:
1 tbsp sunflower oil
500 g (1 lb 2 oz) raw tiger shrimp, peeled
100 g (4 oz) mixed salad leaves (oriental or red stalk leaves)
1 green mango, peeled and flesh cut into fine sticks
½ red pepper, seeded and cut into fine sticks
50 g (2 oz) cucumber, cut into fine sticks
Lime wedges, to garnish

Serves 4

Steamed jumbo shrimp with lemongrass

Ingredients
450 g (1 lb) raw jumbo shrimp
1 stalk of lemongrass,
   quartered lengthways
8 spring onions, trimmed and sliced
2 tbsp coarsely chopped fresh coriander
   leaves
1 red chilli, seeded and thinly sliced

For the sauce:
2 tbsp fish sauce
1 tsp caster sugar
2 tbsp light soy sauce
½ lemongrass stalk, thinly sliced

Serves 4

A light aromatic dish that will appeal to anyone counting their calories. Skinless chicken breasts can also be cooked using the same method below.

Peel the shrimp and cut down the back of each one to remove the dark thread running down its length.

Place the lemongrass in a steamer and arrange the shrimp, spring onions, coriander and red chilli on top. Cover and steam over a saucepan of boiling water for 5 minutes or until the shrimp turn pink.

To make the sauce, mix together the fish sauce, sugar, light soy sauce and lemongrass until the sugar dissolves.

Lift the shrimp, spring onions, coriander and red chilli from the steamer and discard the lemongrass. Serve while still hot with the sauce spooned over.

Yellow chicken curry

*P*erhaps the least known internationally of Thailand's three colour-coded curries – the others being green curry (see page 150) and red curry (see page 159) – this Indian-influenced recipe is very popular in the country's southern region.

Pound all the curry paste ingredients together with a mortar and pestle or in a blender until a fine paste is formed.

Fry the shallots until light brown and set aside.

Heat 225 ml (½ pint) of the coconut milk in a wok or frying pan, add the curry paste and cook for 5 minutes. Add the remaining coconut milk, bring to a boil, add the chicken and cook until tender, for about 10 minutes.

Add the potato and salt, and cook until the potatoes are done, about 10 minutes. Pour into bowls, sprinkle with the fried shallots and garnish with a sprig of kaffir lime. Serve accompanied by ajaad salad (see page 177), sliced pickled ginger and steamed rice.

Ingredients

For the yellow curry paste:
2–3 yellow chillies, chopped
10 small garlic cloves, chopped
½ stalk of lemongrass, sliced
½ tbsp shallots, sliced
2 tsp chilli powder
1 tsp sliced root ginger
1 tsp galangal, sliced
1 tsp shrimp paste (kapi)
1 tsp salt
½ tsp coriander seeds
½ tsp fennel seeds
½ tsp turmeric

For the curry:
3 tbsp sliced shallots
1.5 litres (2½ pints) thin coconut milk
450g (1 lb) chicken, cut into medium-sized
 pieces
200 g (7 oz) potatoes, peeled and cut into
 1-cm (½-in) cubes
2 tsp salt
Sprig of kaffir lime, to garnish

Serves 6

Coconut beef curry

Ingredients

2 tbsp red curry paste (see page 156)

50 ml (2 fl. oz) peanut or corn oil

300 g (11 oz) beef sirloin, cut into
  2.5 x 2 x 0.5-cm (1 x ¾ x ¼-in) slices

900 ml (1½ pints) thin coconut milk

1 tbsp fish sauce

2 tsp sugar

2 fresh red chillies, sliced

2 kaffir lime leaves, sliced finely

75 g (3 oz) Thai basil leaves

Serves 8

*D*espite the addition of coconut milk, this is still one of the driest of all Thai curries, and it is usually quite fiery. If you want to make it less spicy, simply reduce the number of chillies.

Heat the oil in a frying pan or wok and fry the curry paste for 3–4 minutes. Add the beef and fry for a further 2 minutes, then add the coconut milk and simmer until the beef is tender, which should take about 15 minutes.

Add the fish sauce, sugar and chilli. Remove from the heat, transfer to a serving plate and sprinkle with the lime leaves and basil.

Serve in bowls accompanied by steamed rice, pickled vegetables, salted eggs and sun-dried beef.

Southern chilli curry with red and green chillies

*A*s with most of the region's nam priks (spiced dishes), this thick, spicy southern curry is intended to be eaten with plain rice. Don't be fooled by its seeming simplicity; it is both tasty and satisfying, not to mention fairly fiery.

To make the chilli paste, pound all the ingredients together finely with a pestle and mortar or in a food processor.

Boil the water in a pan or wok, add the chilli paste and simmer briefly before adding the pork, fish sauce, curry powder and lime leaf.

Simmer again for 10 minutes before transferring to four serving bowls. Serve accompanied by steamed rice.

Ingredients

For the chilli paste:

8–10 small, dried green and red
    chillies, chopped
6 white peppercorns
2 tbsp shallots, sliced
1 tbsp sliced garlic
1 tsp sliced galangal
1 tsp shrimp paste (kapi)
¼ stalk of lemongrass, sliced

900 ml (1½ pints) water
225 g (8 oz) pork loin, cut into 3 x 2 x 0.5-cm
    (1¼ x ¾ x ¼-in) pieces
3 tbsp fish sauce
1 tsp curry powder
3 kaffir lime leaves, torn into quarters

Serves 4

Whole steamed spiced chicken with a coconut sauce

Ingredients

1.5 kg (3 lb) oven-ready chicken
1 large lemon, halved
2 tsp grated fresh ginger
1 large red chilli, finely chopped
2 garlic cloves, peeled and crushed
2 tsp finely chopped lemongrass
Juice of 1 medium lime
1 tbsp finely chopped fresh coriander
Salt and freshly ground black pepper
½ tsp Thai spice powder (chilli powder, dried garlic, ginger, ground coriander, ground cinnamon, ground cumin, star anise and garlic powder)
2 tbsp vegetable oil
150 ml (5 fl. oz) dry white wine
Kaffir lime leaves

For the sauce:
150 ml (5 fl. oz) coconut milk
150 ml (5 fl. oz) chicken stock

Serves 4

*S*teaming a whole chicken is the perfect way to obtain a really succulent result, and it helps the meat to take on the wonderful Thai flavourings. If lime leaves are unavailable, use large mint or basil leaves. Cooks in Thailand blend their own spice mixes from ingredients bought at the local market. It is, however, possible to buy pre-blended mixtures of Thai spices at specialist southeast Asian food stores.

Wash the chicken inside and out, and pat dry. Place the halved lemon inside the cavity and transfer to a deep glass dish.

Mix the remaining ingredients together (except for the lime leaves) and pour over the chicken. Cover tightly and leave to marinate for at least 2 hours, turning occasionally.

Prepare the steamer, lining the base of the upper tier with the lime leaves. Remove the chicken from the dish, reserving the marinade, and place on top of the lime leaves. Cover and steam for 1–1¼ hours until cooked through.

Meanwhile, heat the marinade in a small saucepan with the stock and coconut milk. Serve with the chicken and steamed fragrant rice (see page 128).

LEFT: A jungle path shaded by coconut groves on Koh Samui, an island of the southeast coast of Thailand.

Fried flat beans with pork

*Y*ou can use fresh lima beans as a substitute for the sator beans, but really the basis for this quintessentially southern dish is the strange flavour of the real thing. The recipe is included here for authenticity and just in case you are able to find the real sator beans in a Thai delicatessen or greengrocer. They are known by various other names, including petai beans, yongchak and the rather unappealing sounding stinky beans.

Pound the chillies and garlic together with a mortar and pestle or whizz in a food processor to a fine paste. Mix with the shrimp paste.

Heat the oil in a frying pan or wok. Add the chilli–garlic mixture, then add the pork and stir-fry for 3 minutes. Add the beans and all the remaining ingredients, plus 3 tablespoons of water if using lima beans. Fry until the beans are cooked. After about 10 minutes they should be quite firm.

Serve accompanied by rice.

Ingredients

3 fresh yellow or green chillies, chopped
1 tbsp chopped garlic
½ tsp shrimp paste (kapi)
2 tbsp peanut or corn oil
150 g (5 oz) pork loin (or chicken or shrimp), cut into thin strips
450 g (1 lb) fresh sator or lima beans
½ tsp fish sauce
½ tsp sugar
½ tsp lime or lemon juice

Serves 4

Fried rice-stick noodles with coconut sauce

Ingredients

275 g (10 oz) dried rice-stick noodles

3 tbsp vegetable oil

2 cloves garlic, finely chopped

3 shallots, chopped

400 g (14 oz) rump steak, thinly sliced

16 canned or fresh baby corn, cut diagonally

4 spring onions, chopped

275 g (10 oz) bean sprouts

700 ml (14 fl. oz) canned coconut milk

2 tsp palm sugar (or dark muscovado sugar)

4 tbsp fish sauce

3 tbsp freshly squeezed lemon juice

1 tbsp red curry paste (see page 156)

Coriander leaves, to garnish

Serves 4

The coconut and its parent palm have a hallowed place in the Thai psyche, and nowhere more so than in the southern region where they grow in abundance. The coconut itself has a wide variety of culinary uses, while the palm is employed to make furniture, toys and musical instruments. Canned coconut milk varies in its consistency depending on the brand. A thicker product produces the richest, smoothest flavour. Remember to shake the can well before opening.

Soak the noodles in warm water for 2–5 minutes, or follow the instructions on the package. Rinse and drain.

Heat the oil in a wok or frying pan, then stir-fry the garlic and shallots for 30 seconds. Add the beef and stir-fry for about 3 minutes, before adding the baby corn, spring onions and bean sprouts.

Add the coconut milk, sugar, fish sauce, lemon juice and curry paste, and stir well until the sauce is absorbed into the noodles.

Arrange the noodles on four plates, sprinkle with coriander leaves and serve at once.

White noodle nests with fish

*T*he basis of this meal-in-a-bowl is a nest of long, thin rice noodles known as khanom chiin, which means 'Chinese noodles'. They are sold in markets thoughout the country and can be purchased in batches of up to a hundred.

Boil the green beans in water for 3–4 minutes, drain, then set aside.

Simmer the fish in a small amount of water for 10 minutes. Remove with a slotted spoon and, when cool, finely chop.

Place the noodles in a pan and pour over boiling water to cover. Bring back to a boil and cook for 5 minutes, then drain. When cool, fold the noodles into four serving bowls.

In a saucepan, heat the coconut milk and chicken stock, then add the chilli paste, fish and fish sauce and boil for 3 minutes. Remove from the heat and spoon over the noodles. Serve with small dishes of bean sprouts, beans, spinach and Thai basil leaves.

Ingredients

175 g (6 oz) chopped green beans
200 g (7 oz) white fish fillets, skinned
225 g (8 oz) dried vermicelli, soaked for
3–5 minutes
900 ml (1½ pints) coconut milk
900 ml (1½ pints) chicken stock
100 ml (4 fl. oz) red chilli paste (see page 51)
3 tbsp fish sauce
100 g (4 oz) bean sprouts, blanched
100 g (4 oz) spinach, blanched
100 g (4 oz) Thai basil leaves

Serves 4

Chilli preserve

There are probably as many recipes in Thailand for chilli preserve as there are cooks, but the common ingredient in all of them is the large dried red chillies available from Thai food stores or other Asian food stores. Fresh chillies will not give the same intense flavour and colour and their extra fluid will prevent the preserve from becoming thick and sticky.

Ingredients
15 g (½ oz) large dried red chillies
Peanut oil for deep-frying
1 red pepper, seeded and chopped
4 purple shallots, peeled and chopped
2 cloves garlic, peeled and chopped
225 g (8 oz) canned chopped tomatoes
1 tsp shrimp paste (kapi)
2 tbsp soft brown sugar
50 ml (2 fl. oz) fish sauce

Makes about 12 fl. oz

Place the chillies in a bowl, cover with hot water, and leave to soak for 30 minutes. Drain, split open and remove the seeds.

Heat the oil for deep-frying in a wok and deep-fry the chillies for a couple of minutes until they are dark red. Drain on paper towel.

Discard all but 2 tablespoons of the oil, add the red pepper and shallots to the pan and fry for around 5 minutes. Add the garlic, fry for a further 2 minutes, and then stir in the tomatoes, chillies and shrimp paste.

Lower the heat and simmer gently for 30 minutes. Cool a little, then purée in a food processor with the sugar and fish sauce.

Return the purée to the wok and cook it very gently for about 40 minutes until dark, caramelized and jelly-like in consistency, stirring regularly so it does not stick to the pan and burn.

Crisp fried fish with chilli preserve

*K*nown *in Thailand as pra tod lard prik, this recipe works best if you add yeast to the batter mix as it will give the fish a wonderfully crisp, light coating that will not go soggy after frying. To activate the yeast effectively, it is important to stir it thoroughly into the flour before adding the liquid. The recipe can be prepared with any firm white fish. If using a flat fish, such as sole or flounder, cut the fillets into fairly wide strips and reduce the frying time to 2–3 minutes.*

Sprinkle the yeast and sugar over the flour in a bowl and stir well. Add the water and mix with a wooden spoon to make a smooth batter. Cover and leave for 1 hour until frothy.

Heat the oil for deep-frying in a wok or large saucepan to 180°C (350°F), or until a cube of bread dropped into it turns golden in 60 seconds. Stir the fresh coriander into the batter.

Coast the fish pieces in the seasoned flour and dip into the batter until coated.

Fry a few pieces at a time in the hot oil for about 5 minutes or until golden brown and crisp. Drain on paper towel and keep warm while you fry the rest.

Serve the fish garnished with lime wedges for squeezing over the fish, and accompanied by chilli preserve.

Ingredients

7 g (¼ oz) dry yeast

Pinch of sugar

175 g (6 oz) plain flour, plus extra seasoned flour to coat the fish

150 ml (5 fl. oz) tepid water

Peanut or vegetable oil for deep-frying

1 tbsp chopped fresh coriander

550 g (1¼ lb) firm white fish fillets, such as monkfish, sea bass, or cod, cut into 6-cm (2-in) pieces

Lime wedges, to garnish

Chilli preserve (see opposite), to serve

Serves 4

Salmon steaks in peanut and chilli sauce

Ingredients

4 salmon steaks, about 175 g (6 oz) each
1 small onion, sliced
2 bay leaves
Few sprigs of parsley
4–5 peppercorns
100 ml (4 fl. oz) dry white wine
1 tbsp white wine vinegar
50 ml (2 fl. oz) water

Fo the sauce:
2 tbsp olive oil
1 garlic clove, crushed
2.5-cm (1-in) piece root ginger, peeled and grated
100 g (4 oz) raw peanuts, shelled
2 red chillies, seeded and sliced
2 tsp soft dark brown sugar
225 ml (8 fl. oz) vegetable stock
1 tbsp lemon juice
Lemon slices to garnish

Serves 4

*T*his recipe features three of the most popular ingredients in southern Thai cooking: fresh fish, peanuts and fiery hot chillies.

Wipe the salmon and reserve. Place the onion, bay leaves, parsley, peppercorns, wine and vinegar in a frying pan. Add the water and leave to boil. Reduce the heat and simmer for 10 minutes. Strain and reserve the liquid until ready to cook the fish.

Heat the oil for the sauce in the frying pan and fry the garlic and ginger for 2 minutes. Add the peanuts and fry gently for 10 minutes, or until golden.

Put the peanuts, garlic, ginger and oil, along with the remaining sauce ingredients, in a food processor. Blend to a purée, then return to the cleaned pan and simmer for 8–10 minutes, or until reduced slightly. Keep warm while cooking the fish.

When ready to cook the fish, reheat the reserved liquid in the frying pan and add the fish. Bring to a boil, then cover and reduce the heat to a very gently simmer. Cook for 3–4 minutes, or until the fish is cooked. Drain and arrange on serving plates and spoon over a little sauce. Garnish with lemon slices.

LEFT: Squid caught in Chumpon, southern Thailand, hanging out to dry above a sheltered bay.

Coconut custard

In Thailand, coconut milk is often used to make a sweet, creamy custard known as sankhaya, which is cooked in a double boiler and then a steamer to prevent bubbles forming in the custard. Canned Thai coconut milk is the right consistency for the recipe but because cream tends to settle on the top, the milk needs a good stir or a quick whizz in a food processor to restore its smooth texture. Take care not to allow the custard to boil or it will curdle. If this does happen, remove the saucepan from the heat and strain, or process the custard in a food processor until smooth again.

Ingredients
2 large eggs, lightly beaten
50 g (2 oz) white sugar
225 ml (8 fl. oz) thick canned coconut milk
Few drops of vanilla extract

Makes 4

Whisk the eggs and sugar together until creamy, then stir in the coconut milk until evenly blended.

Strain into a double boiler set over a pan of boiling water and cook gently, stirring constantly, until the mixture coats the back of a wooden spoon. Stir in the vanilla and pour the custard into four small bowls or ramekins. Cover lightly with foil and steam over just-simmering water for 15 minutes or until the custards are just set. Let cool.

Coconut custard with spiced fruit salad

*M*ost meals in Thailand end not with a dessert but with a platter of the many luscious fruits that grow all over the country. In this recipe, the coconut custard is served with a fresh fruit salad lightly spiced with cinnamon, star anise and cloves. If you want to spice things up a bit more, add a little grated fresh root ginger, bruised lemongrass stalk or split vanilla bean to the pineapple juice. If rambutans are not available, lychees can be substituted. You might also like to dust the top of the custards with a little ground cinnamon before serving.

Place the pineapple juice in a small pan, add the star anise, cinnamon and cloves and bring to a simmering point. Remove from the heat and set aside to cool.

Pile the prepared fruit in a serving bowl and pour the spiced juice over it. Chill until ready to serve.

Spoon the fruit salad onto serving plates, with the small bowls of custard on the side.

Ingredients

300 ml (10 fl. oz) pineapple juice

2 star anise

1 cinnamon stick, broken into short lengths

4 cloves

1 mango, peeled and sliced

½ papaya, peeled, seeded and chopped

1 slice pineapple, cut into small pieces

4 rambutans, peeled, pitted and halved

1 star fruit, sliced

Seeds from ½ pomegranate

4 coconut custards (see opposite)

Serves 4

Banana and pineapple fritters in coconut batter

*T*his is a popular street snack in Thailand where roadside chefs toss the crisp fritters in woks of sizzling oil. If using canned pineapple, drain it well and blot away any juice with a paper towel before coating with the batter. Use slightly under-ripe bananas so they do not become too soft when cooked.

Sift the flour and ginger into a bowl and stir in the sugar. Make a well in the centre of the dry ingredients and pour in the coconut milk. Whisk to make a smooth batter, and then set aside for 30 minutes.

Heat the peanut oil for deep-frying at 180°C (350°F), or until a cube of bread dropped in turns golden after 60 seconds.

Dust the banana and pineapple pieces with flour, dip in the batter until coated, and deep-fry in batches for 2–3 minutes until golden and crisp. Drain on paper towel and serve scattered with shredded or desiccated coconut, or coconut ice cream.

Ingredients

225 g (8 oz) plain flour, plus extra for dusting
½ tsp ground ginger
50 g (2 oz) caster sugar
225 ml (8 fl. oz) coconut milk
Peanut oil, for deep-frying
2 bananas, peeled and
    cut into 5-cm (2-in) lengths
2 pineapple rings, quartered
Shredded young coconut
    or desiccated coconut, or coconut
    icecream

Serves 4

Coconut jelly

Ingredients

4 sheets of leaf gelatine

175 ml (6 fl. oz) coconut milk

175 ml (6 fl. oz) water

50 g (2 oz) caster sugar

50 g (2 oz) young coconut, grated

Toasted grated fresh or desiccated coconut

Makes 20

*S*erve this cut up into small pieces as it is rich and very sweet. Be sure to stir the gelatine until it is fully dissolved to give the jelly a lovely smooth texture.

Soak the gelatine leaves in a little cold water for 5 minutes to soften. Remove and squeeze them out.

Heat the coconut milk, water and sugar in a saucepan until almost boiling, add the gelatine leaves, and stir until dissolved.

Add the grated coconut, pour into a shallow tray lined with clingfilm and allow to cool. Chill until set.

Serve the jelly cut into small triangles, squares or flower shapes using a fluted cutter, and scatter with toasted, grated fresh or desiccated coconut.

Index

banana and pineapple fritters in coconut batter 218

beans:
curried fried rice with green haricot beans 57
fried flat with pork 206
green bean salad with shallot croutons 51

beef:
and rocket salad 48
coconut beef curry 201
green beef curry 151
grilled, salad with fish sauce, herb and lime dressing 114
raw beef salad 91
spicy egg noodles with beef and vegetables 78
boar: wild boar country curry 117

chicken:
barbecue with chilli vinegar sauce 60
Chiang Mai noodles with 96
chicken, aubergine and noodle broth 31
coconut and galangal soup 174
crisp fried rice vermicelli 71
crispy fried rice vermicelli with garlic, fish sauce and lime stir-fry sauce 73
curried noodles 95
fried rice with onion and garlic 56
green curry with 155
mango, and rice salad 47
Northern Thai chicken curry with red chillies 92
pad thai 64
with peppers and bean-thread noodles 74
and pineapple with three-flavor sauce 63
and pomelo salad with fresh coriander, lime and green chilli dressing 143
satay 177
spicy rice-stick noodles with 66
sweet and sour 163
with Thai basil 59

whole steamed spiced with coconut sauce 205
yellow chicken curry 198

chilli 20:
relish 40
sauce 181, 185, 215
vinegar: crab cakes with 137
vinegar sauce 60
preserve 212, 213

coconut:
custard 216
and galangal soup 174
jelly 221
rice salad with roasted 52
sauce 205, 209

crab:
cakes with chilli vinegar 137
crab, pomelo and rice noodle salad 110
and mangetout salad 141
stuffed crab shells 140

curries:
coconut beef 201
colour-coded 22
curried fried rice with haricot beans 57
curried noodles 95
green beef 151
green with chicken 155
Northern Thai chicken with red chillies 92
Northern Thai pork 93
red vegetable with sweet potato 160
Southern with chillies 202
wild boar country 117
yellow chicken 198

festival foods 24-5

fish:
crisp fried with chilli preserve 213
white noodle nests with fish 210
fish: fried, spicy salad 113

fish cakes:
spicy with coriander soy dipping sauce 186
with sweet chilli dipping sauce 185
flat breads 100

fruit 24
salad with lime and papaya sauce 124
garlic, chilli and lime dressing 147
ginger dressing 106
green curry paste 150
greens, stir-fried 42
hors d'oeuvre, Thai 43

lemongrass and lime mousse 83
lime and papaya sauce 124
lime-marinated pork skewers 39

mango:
coconut sticky rice with mango, papaya and lime 123
green papaya salad with lemongrass, coriander and ginger dressing 106
rice, mango and shrimp salad with lemongrass dressing 144
salsa 28
sorbet 80
meat and tomato dip, spicy 893
mousse, lemongrass and lime 83

mussels:
fried mussel pancakes 138
and shrimp fritters 190
spicy mussel salad 148

noodles:
casseroled shrimp with bean-thread noodles 165
chicken, aubergine and noodle broth 31
chicken pad thai 64
chicken with peppers and bean-thread noodles 74
crab, pomelo and rice noodle salad 110
crisp fried rice vermicelli 71, 73
curried 95
egg noodles with tofu and vegetables 79
fried bean-thread noodles with tofu 77
fried rice noodles with chillies and vegetables 65
fried rice-stick 164 , 209

hot and sour noodle soup with shrimp 131
and Chinese cabbage salad in a peanut
   dressing 55
rice-stick with pork and shrimp 69
spicy egg noodles with beef and
   vegetables 78
spicy noodle salad with shrimp 120
spicy rice-stick with chicken 66
white noodle nests with fish 210
Northern Thai soup 90

pad thai 22
   chicken 64
pancakes, fried mussel 138
peanut:
   dressing 55, 182
   sauce 178
pork:
   Chiang Mai sausages 99
   clear soup with stuffed mushrooms 35
   crisp fried rice vermicelli 71
   crispy fried rice vermicelli with garlic, fish
     sauce and lime stir-fry sauce 73
   fried flat beans with 206
   green papaya salad with lemongrass,
     cilantro and ginger dressing 106
   lime-marinated pork skewers 39
   and noodle soup 132
   Northern Thai pork curry 93
   Northern Thai soup 90
   rice-stick noodles with pork and shrimp 69
   spicy pork curry 119
   stuffed baby squid in a broth 133
   sweet crisp-fried vermicelli with shrimp,
     pork and tofu 167

rice 18-19, 21
   chicken fried rice with onion and garlic 56
   chicken, mango and rice salad 47
   curried fried rice with haricot beans 57
   mango and shrimp salad with lemongrass
     dressing 144
   salad with roasted coconut 52

shrimp skewers with coconut 189
steamed 128
see also sticky rice
rice-stick noodles with pork and shrimp 69

salads 23
   beef and rocket 48
   chicken, mango and rice 47
   chicken and pomelo salad with fresh
     coriander, lime and chilli dressing 143
   crab, pomelo and rice noodle 110
   fruit with lime and papaya sauce 124
   green bean with shallot croûtons 51
   green papaya with lemongrass, coriander
     and ginger dressing 106
   grilled beef with fish sauce, herb and lime
     dressing 114
   lime-dressed shrimp 194
   noodles and Chinese cabbage in a peanut
     dressing 55
   rice, mango, and shrimp with lemongrass
     dressing 144
   spiced fruit 217
   spicy green papaya and vegetable 109
   spicy mussel 148
   spicy noodle with shrimp 120
   spicy seafood with sea bass 193
   tofu in garlic, chilli and lime dressing 147
satay sauce 177
sausages, Chiang Mai 99
scallops:
   with lemongrass broth and spinach 134
   with Thai basil, coriander and garlic 149
   seafood salad, spicy, with sea bass 193
shrimp:
   casseroled with bean-thread noodles 165
   crisp fried rice vermicelli 71
   fried rice-stick noodles with 164
   green curry with shrimp, pumpkin and
     courgette 152
   hot and sour noodle soup with 131
   lime-dressed, salad 194
   mussel and shrimp fritters 190

rice, mango and shrimp salad with
   lemongrass dressing 144
skewers with coconut rice 189
spicy noodle salad with 120
steamed jumbo with lemongrass 197
sweet crisp-fried vermicelli with shrimp
   and cashew nuts 166
sorbet, mango 80
soups:
   clear with stuffed mushrooms 35
   coconut and galangal 174
   hot and sour noodle with shrimp 131
   Northern Thai 90
   pork and noodle 132
   spiced chicken 32
   spices 20
   spinach scallops with lemongrass broth 134
   squid: stuffed baby squid in a broth 133
sticky rice 86
stir-fry sauce, lime 73
swordfish, grilled, with lime and cilantro 169

techniques 18-19
tempeh:
   deep-fried with sweet chilli sauce 181
   and vegetable salad with peanut dressing
     182
three-flavour sauce 63
tofu:
   egg noodles with tofu and vegetables 79
   fried bean-thread noodles with 77
   red curry with 159

vegetables:
   fried rice noodles with chillies and 65
   mini vegetable and herb rolls 36
   spicy green papaya and vegetable salad
     109
   Thai 44
   vegetable fritters with chilli relish 40
vine leaves: Thai hors d'oeuvre 43

yum nua 23

Picture credits

The images in this book are used with the permission of the copyright holders stated below. (Images are listed by page number.) All other illustrations and pictures are © Quintet Publishing Limited. While every effort has been made to credit contributors, Quintet would like to apologize should there have been any omissions or errors and would be pleased to make the appropriate correction for future editions of the book.